Lovable Racists,
Magical Negroes, and
White Messiahs

Lovable Racists, Magical Negroes, and White Messiahs

DAVID IKARD

With a Foreword by T. Denean Sharpley-Whiting

The University of Chicago Press   Chicago and London

The University of Chicago Press, Chicago 60637
The University of Chicago Press, Ltd., London
© 2017 by The University of Chicago
Published 2017
Printed in the United States of America

26 25 24 23 22 21 20 19 18 17   1 2 3 4 5

ISBN-13: 978-0-226-49246-9 (cloth)
ISBN-13: 978-0-226-49263-6 (paper)
ISBN-13: 978-0-226-49277-3 (e-book)
DOI: 10.7208/chicago/9780226492773.001.0001

Library of Congress Cataloging-in-Publication Data

Names: Ikard, David, 1972– author. | Sharpley-Whiting, T. Denean,
    writer of foreword.
Title: Lovable racists, magical negroes, and white messiahs / David Ikard ;
    with a foreword by T. Denean Sharpley-Whiting.
Description: Chicago ; London : The University of Chicago Press, 2017. |
    Includes bibliographical references and index.
Identifiers: LCCN 2017003728 | ISBN 9780226492469 (cloth : alk. paper) |
    ISBN 9780226492636 (pbk. : alk. paper) | ISBN 9780226492773
    (e-book)
Subjects: LCSH: United States—Race relations. | Racism—United States. |
    African Americans—Social conditions. | Slavery—United States.
Classification: LCC E185.625 .I38 2017 | DDC 305.800973—dc23
    LC record available at https://lccn.loc.gov/2017003728

♾ This paper meets the requirements of ANSI/NISO Z39.48-1992
(Permanence of Paper).

Contents

Acknowledgments

I started writing this book right around the time that Trayvon Martin was killed. I distinctly remember how the mainstream media trivialized the case to such an extent that the national conversation became about gangsta rap and black urban dress codes. Even though I frankly didn't expect Martin to receive justice (remember it took a major groundswell of protest to even pressure the district attorney to charge Martin's killer, George Zimmerman, with murder), I was still rocked by the trial and the not-guilty verdict. Since that moment, many hundreds more have been unjustly murdered by the police or those acting as patrollers. Several of the victims have reached cultural martyr status, including Michael Brown, Eric Garner, Sandra Bland (yes, I think she was murdered), Tamir Rice, John Crawford, Laquan McDonald, Philando Castile, Alton Sterling, Corey Jones, and Korryn Gaines. And then there was white supremacist Dylan Roof who walked into a black church in South Carolina and slaughtered nine innocent souls, hoping to start a race war.

Suffice it to say, as I was writing this book America felt like it was on fire—as though the clock was being turned back on civil rights. And in some sense our country was literally on fire. Ferguson and Baltimore erupted in flames as rebellions to police brutality and terrorism grew. The national mood was souring and the police were doubling down on their right to employ whatever means necessary to maintain dominance and control. Police unions were even trying to silence outspoken celebrities like Beyoncé Knowles and Kendrick Lamar by threatening to boycott their events and deny security details.

However idealistic it may sound, I feel that I have been called to a special purpose; that for some unbeknownst reason, the universe bestowed this working-class country boy from North Carolina with gifts of writerly expression and intellect. I write with the political conviction that my words not only matter but have the power to transform social realities. There were many times, however, during the writing of this book that I lost that conviction; that I feared my efforts were in vain; that my critique of willful white ignorance would fall on deaf ears.

Thankfully, I have a village of friends, colleagues, and family that I can rely on to encourage me when I need encouraging, to challenge me when I need challenging, to console me when I need consoling, and to uplift me when I need uplifting. One of my biggest supporters in this village is my best friend and ace boon coon, Martell Teasley. He keeps me honest and on track. I lean heavily on his wise counsel. Much love also goes out to Tracy Sharpley-Whiting. Beyond being a bomb-ass intellectual of the first order, "Trace" is one of the kindest, most giving individuals I know. I am proud to have her as a role model and friend. To quote my homeboy Tupac, "You are appreciated." There are people in my village that I don't get to talk to on a regular basis but who are nevertheless major inspirations in my life. These folks include Wizdom Powell Brown, Rhea Lathan, Hope Ealey, Wanda Costen, Calvin Hall, Lisa Thompson, Lisa Woolfork, Rayshawn Ray, Monica Coleman, La Vinia Jennings, Donette Francis, Georgette Spratling and her lovely daughter Brie, Jeffery McCune, and Janice Johnson.

I also want to shout out my fantastic past and present students, including Regina Bradley, La-Toya Scott (aka green banana), Joshua Burnett, Nicole Carr, Jonquil Bailey, Hicham Mazouz, and Allison Nicole Harris. Y'all make me so proud!

My family is certainly a crucial part of my village. Shout out to Joan Ikard (aka mom) and Harold Ikard (aka pops). Shout out to my five siblings: Regina, Tiffany, Crystal, Randy, and Terry. Love to my beautiful, super-talented niece JaKayla and my dynamic, handsome nephews Jamar, Christopher, Damian, and Tyrell (RIP).

It is my great fortune to be the father of two incredible human beings in Elijah and Octavia Ikard. They fill me with unspeakable joy. Watching them transition from childhood to young adulthood has been amazing. They will accomplish much in this world.

The fact that I was able to push past the obstacles—emotional and otherwise—and produce this book is a direct testament to the power of this incredible village of support. I love you all and thank you for looking out for a brotha. The grind is real but so is the love and support.

Racial Realism Redux

There has been of late a lot said and written about whiteness. How it dovetails, for instance, with gender in the formation of what some have cheekily dubbed the phenomenon of "white women's tears" that ably obviate charges of racism (see Mamta Motwani Accapadi's essay "When White Women Cry" and Robin DiAngelo's "White Women's Tears and the Men Who Love Them"). This sociocultural diagnosis falls under the general condition of "white fragility" as deftly laid out by DiAngelo and mined to good effect in David Ikard's *Lovable Racists, Magical Negroes, and White Messiahs.*

Through the labyrinth of visual, sport, and political cultures and literary studies that his wordsmithing and analyses cut through with scalpel-like precision, Ikard reaches destination "racial realism,"[1] in the words of the late legal scholar Derrick Bell. That is, that white antiblack racism in all of its forms—murderous and benign—is not an infectious carbuncle on an otherwise healthy body politic. Rather, the contagious excrescence is a necessary, permanent, and lethal—given continued racialized state violence in the twenty-first century—fixture of American society. America's original sin of slavery, the greatest betrayal as totted up by Bell, created a symbiosis between racism and that experiment in democracy called America at its founding in the eighteenth century. While the primary author of the *Federalist Papers*, Alexander Hamilton, connived for slavery's abolition, he ran up against a powerful Virginia block of Founding Fathers in the form of Thomas Jefferson and James Madison—elite slaveholders posing as gentlemen farmers.

At the center of this symbiosis rooted in slavery is not blackness alone—though it is an "immovable star" in the worldview of most white Americans, but historically shifting ideas of whiteness. As Nell Painter writes in her *History of White People*: "Slavery has helped construct concepts of white race in . . . contradictory ways."[2] Painter elaborates on the historical reality of unfree whites—white slavery—as well as black slavery and their uses in structuring race, racial difference discrimination, and white identity in the newly formed nation and continuing on into our present reality.

Ikard, for his part, conceptually runs with this pass, to use a sports metaphor, throughout *Lovable Racists*. In doing so, he joins a long list of intellectuals in plumbing race and racism's transmogrifications in popular culture and in the hoity-toity, seemingly enlightened realm of literary high culture. From James Baldwin's palpable scorn at white innocence (a version of white fragility) in *The Fire Next Time*, to Toni Morrison's taking apart the canonical literature of Young America to unveil variations of whiteness highly dependent on immovable blackness, to Karen and Barbara Fields's study of the craftiness of race and philosopher Naomi Zack's rejection of the term "white privilege" while parsing black rights, to Shannon Sullivan's exploration of good white people and flawed, middle-class white antiracism.

Intellectual manna, yet teeth-gnashing reads. And Ikard's, no less. There were times when I desperately availed myself of a tea break to soothe my fits of pique. But one must concede that there is something edifying, productive even, in working through the varied, complicated, unbearable, and burdened being of whiteness—in Rudyard Kipling's nous. *Lovable Racists* serves as both guidepost and road map.

—T. Denean Sharpley-Whiting
Nashville, Tennessee

Introduction

[Whites] have organized society to reproduce and reinforce our racial interests and perspectives. Further, we are centered in all matters deemed normal, universal, benign, neutral and good. Thus, we move through a wholly racialized world with an unracialized identity (e.g. white people can represent all of humanity, people of color can only represent their racial selves). Challenges to this identity become highly stressful and even intolerable. ROBIN DIANGELO

As an unapologetic and outspoken scholar-activist who writes extensively about racism, white supremacy, black popular culture, presidential politics, gender politics, and sexuality, I am certainly no stranger to controversy. Moreover, I inherited the personality of my mother, Joan Ikard: which is to say I do not shirk from confrontation and have a deep and abiding passion for social justice, especially when it comes to black folks. Indeed, when it comes to confronting social injustice and specifically racial inequality, "my moms ain't scerd," as the African American colloquialism goes, and neither is her eldest son. But what happened during a 2014 lecture and book-signing event in Miami for my third book, *Blinded by the Whites: Why Race Still Matters in 21st -Century America*, set me on my heels because frankly I did not see it coming. The lecture/book signing was at a local and beloved bookstore in Coral Gables; the clientele decidedly white, upper-class, and politically liberal. Those who attended the academic lectures that the bookstore frequently hosted tended to be even more leftist than the general clientele. In a word, I expected my crowd to be at least sophisticated enough not to make blatantly racialist comments or have the wherewithal to try to mask them.

The informed and insightful comments I fielded during the question-and-answer session of my lecture made me feel even more at ease. I was abruptly rocked out of my racial comfort zone when I began to sign books, however. As I was having an engaging conversation with a young white elementary school teacher who had read my book and was sharing her challenges with discussing racism with her students in her test-happy conservative public school environment in Florida, a rather large and aggressive middle-aged white man (at least six feet four inches tall and weighing well over two hundred pounds) inserted himself into the conversation: "Excuse me, I hate to interrupt, but it was Niggers with Attitudes not Niggers for Life? NWA, the group you referenced in your talk, stands for Niggers with Attitudes. You got your facts wrong in your lecture!" My initial reaction was stunned silence. I noticed that the teacher was visibly stunned too. She stepped back abruptly and put her hand nervously over her mouth. Hearing the word "nigger" used so freely and with such simmering anger and entitlement (and, quite frankly, feeling as if his vehement invocation of the word was a veiled way to call me a "nigger"), I was swept up in intense emotions. Though I am not one of those black folks that typically make a distinction between "niggers" and "niggaz" (which is actually what the "N" in NWA stands for) because to my mind they are both epithets and should be treated as such (some blacks argue that the former is the offensive term and the latter is a term of endearment reserved for blacks only), I was emotionally struck by the fact that my white confronter had used the former pronunciation, which triggered painful memories of my southern childhood, where the epithet was frequently wielded as a weapon by whites, including some of my grade-school teachers. The last time I recall being confronted in such a direct and venomous manner was in 1986, my freshman year in high school, when I tangled with a white male student who was surreptitiously passing out Ku Klux Klan applications to select white students during lunch. A physical altercation nearly ensued.

When I gathered my wits enough to respond to this angry white man, I said, "Excuse me, who are you exactly?" He introduced himself as a professor in one of the liberal arts departments at the University of Miami, where I had just accepted a position. I learned later that he was also an award-winning independent filmmaker. His beef with my book lecture—at least the one that he felt empowered to articulate—was based on his ignorance about hip hop and African American popular culture. During my talk I had referenced the gangsta rap group NWA and their 1991 blockbuster album "Niggaz4Life" (also known as "EfiL4zaggin") to underscore the ways that white corporate America (upon learning that the highly sought after middle-class white demographic in the 18–34 age range was listening to hip hop and especially gangsta rap) imposed its will on the music, trying to brand the most problematic aspects of gangsta rap, including misogyny, hypermaterialism, drug dealing, and gang violence, as *the* authentic expression of hip hop music and, by extension, "blackness." Invoking Byron Hurt's brilliant documentary *Beyond Beats and Rhymes* and Tricia Rose's illuminating book *Hip Hop Wars*, I further added that the version of gangsta rap that white corporate America peddled, with the help of some opportunist black executives and desperate artists, was stripped almost entirely of its political critique of police brutality, poverty, and white supremacy and, by turn, its celebration of black empowerment, self-determination, and community uplift. The thing is, the thrust of my talk was about the new iterations of white supremacy in the forms of postracialism, colorblindness, neoliberalism, and what Michelle Alexander calls the "New Jim Crow" that I explore in *Blinded by the Whites*. I broached the issue of white corporate America's takeover, rebranding, and pathologizing of blackness vis-à-vis hip hop music to highlight how white supremacist capitalism, under the guises of promoting free speech and empowering black artists to "speak their truth," even colonizes the spaces and modes of black representation and self-expression. The reference to NWA and "Niggaz4Life" was actually not in my prepared remarks. It came to mind as I was reading my script; I referenced it extemporaneously to give the audience an example of what I was trying to elucidate in the book about the shifting dynamics of white supremacist capitalism over the past few decades and the political stakes therein for black folks. The part of my lecture that *supposedly* stirred my white colleague to confront and correct me had to do with the fact that he was not familiar with the title of NWA's final album "Niggaz4Life" and thus thought I was referring to the group Niggaz With Attitudes as "Niggaz4Life." I put supposedly in italics because my sense is that, at bottom, he was actually upset with the audacity of my claim that even most progressive (middle- and upper-class) white liberals have a deep and abiding investment in certain aspects of white supremacy and, by extension, institutionalized racial inequality.

In her groundbreaking essay "White Fragility," white social science scholar Robin DiAngelo exposes the problems of such "fragile" white egos, including why even the slightest black/brown invocation of white supremacy is so threatening to white identity. She coined the term white fragility to register the problematic ways whites react when people of color pose challenges to their white supremacist entitlements. These challenges include "choosing not to protect the racial feelings of white people," "suggesting that a white person's viewpoint comes from a racialized frame of reference," and "receiving feedback that one's behavior had a racist impact."[1] DiAngelo argues that the typical white response to these challenges (which most whites encounter with little frequency) is to "withdraw, defend, cry, argue, minimize, ignore, and in other ways push back to regain our racial position [of authority over the person of color posing the challenge] and equilibrium." She expounds: "Socialized into a deeply internalized sense of superiority and entitlement that we are either not consciously aware of or can never admit to ourselves, we become highly fragile in conversations about race. We experience a challenge to our racial worldview as a challenge to our very identities as good, moral people. It also challenges our sense of rightful place in the hierarchy. Thus, we perceive any attempt to connect us to the system of racism as a very unsettling and unfair moral offense."[2]

DiAngelo makes clear that whites who identify as liberal are actually *more* threatened by such black/brown invocations of their white privilege than whites who identify as conservative. The reason for this is that, unlike conservative-minded whites, liberal-identified whites experience their antiracist reputations as cultural currency. Thus when black/brown folks threaten this currency by pressing them to acknowledge their white privilege, liberal-identified whites will often prioritize protecting "what they perceive as their moral reputations . . . rather than recognize or change their participation in systems of inequity and domination."[3]

I got to experience this liberal-minded white fragility when I made it clear to the professor who challenged me at the lecture that I was deeply offended by both his aggressive, paternalistic, and condescending approach and his liberal use of the word "nigger." Rather than apologize or acknowledge any wrongdoing, he insisted that I had misunderstood his intent even as he lowered his tone and took a step back from me. (His loud admonishment had actually attracted a small crowd.) He then spent the next few minutes, just as aggressively, running down his résumé of antiracist and progressive activities to disabuse me of what I am sure he assumed was my perception of him as a racist. In fact, he couched his initial assault as an effort to "help" me; he sought to correct my supposed error about NWA out of the same concerning impulse one would alert their friend to brush off dandruff on their shoulder or to remove a food particle from their teeth. He was doing me a favor—saving me from public embarrassment. Ergo I should have responded with gratitude, not attitude. He was, after all, a good antiracist white liberal, not to be confused with the whites I critiqued in my lecture who were consciously and unconsciously invested in white supremacist thinking and institutionalized racial inequality. Alas, he was offended by my audacity to be offended by his words and, by turn, my seeming unwillingness to distinguish him as a good white antiracist liberal and racial ally.

Tellingly, it never seemed to occur to him to acknowledge that he was out of line; that he had overstepped his bounds intellectually (after all, his corrective gesture turned out to expose his ignorance); that he had offended me with his ill-advised and repeated use of nigger; that he could have squashed a lot of the mess that he had created in that moment by simply apologizing. Of course the reason these things never occurred to him was because, based on his reaction and rhetoric, he viewed himself as what Brit Bennett calls "Good White People." In her op-ed "I Don't Know What to Do with Good White People," Bennett describes "good white people" as liberal whites who have the "decency" to acknowledge white privilege but only in the most self-serving of ways. Referencing the response of many good white people to the killing of Michael Brown and Eric Garner, she avers, "I've seen good white people congratulate themselves for deleting racist friends from Facebook or debating family members or performing small acts of kindness to Black people. Sometimes I think I'd prefer racist trolling to this grade of self-aggrandizement. A racist troll is easy to dismiss. He does not think decency is enough. Sometimes I think good white people expect to be rewarded for their decency. We are not like those other white people. See how enlightened and aware we are? See how good?"[4] Bennett not only identifies the quid pro quo nature of white empathy but shows how ostensible gestures of white goodwill and good intentions reproduce white supremacy in the expectations of, if not demands for, black gratitude. Denying this reciprocity of gratitude or, better yet, having the audacity to call these largely vacuous gestures of white empathy into question and demanding more accountability from whites, including dismantling the institutions of power that regulate extant racial inequalities, is not allowed for in this quid pro quo relationship and indeed can get the audacious black agent into a whole heap of trouble.

In his landmark study *Racism without Racists*, Eduardo Bonilla-Silva puts a finer point on this debate about white good intentions and culpability in oppression. He reminds us that white good intentions often operate in concert with white supremacist ideology: "Historically, many good people supported slavery and Jim Crow. Similarly, most color-blind whites who oppose (or have serious reservations about) affirmative action, believe that blacks' problems are mostly their own doing, and do not see anything wrong with their own white lifestyle are good people, too."[5] The crucial analytical issue for Bonilla-Silva "is examining how many whites subscribe to an ideology that ultimately helps preserve racial inequality."[6] Efforts to assess the percentage of whites who hate or love blacks and other systemically marginalized groups or whether they are sincere in their assessments of black struggles, self-determination, meritocracy, and white privilege are intellectually bankrupt. Internalized white supremacy coupled with orchestrated and policed material realities that reinforce status quo racialist thinking encourage warped racial reasoning. It should come as no surprise then that racists cannot only be "good people" but also incredibly sincere in their racist reasoning.

Ta-Nehisi Coates expounds on this phenomenon of white racist sincerity in his op-ed "The Good Racist People." As the provocative title clearly indicates, our white supremacist–minded society allows whites to be deeply invested in white supremacy and still be ultimately perceived in the public domain as good, moral people. To underscore this point, Coates references a deli in Manhattan he once enthusiastically patronized that humiliated actor Forest Whitaker when one of its white employees accused him of stealing and then frisked him like a cop, searching for the items he supposedly stole. When the news of this high-profile blunder broke, the white owner of the deli apologized profusely but (mis)represented the assault as an "honest mistake made by a decent man who was just doing his job."[7] Coates opines that he did not believe the white store owner was being disingenuous. That is to say, he believes that the store owner experienced the incident as a genuine misunderstanding. The problem is that everyday racism is so commonplace—which is to say that it is reinforced socially, economically, and politically in how white apparatuses of power like the police forces, judicial systems, and corporate America pathologize and devalue black humanity—that many whites are encouraged either to be blind to everyday racism or to misidentify it as harmless.

The unuttered racial mindset is that blacks are prone to criminal and pathological behavior so whites that occasionally confuse the minority of upstanding, law-abiding blacks with the "majority" of criminal-minded blacks are hardly racist. At worst, they are overly cautious. Because of this social and racial phenomenon, the only racists appear to be extreme and monstrous. Coates explains, "In modern America we believe racism to be the property of the uniquely villainous and morally deformed, the ideology of trolls, gorgons and orcs. We believe this even when we are actually being racist. In 1957, neighbors in Levittown, Pa., uniting under the flag of segregation, wrote: 'As moral, religious and law-abiding citizens, we feel that we are unprejudiced and undiscriminating in our wish to keep our community a closed community.'" He further notes,

The idea that racism lives in the heart of particularly evil individuals, as opposed to the heart of a democratic society, is reinforcing to anyone who might, from time to time, find their tongue sprinting ahead of their discretion. We can forgive Whitaker's assailant. Much harder to forgive is all that makes Whitaker stand out in the first place. . . . The promise of America is that those who play by the rules, who observe the norms of the 'middle class,' will be treated as such. But this injunction is only half-enforced when it comes to black people, in large part because we were never meant to be part of the American story. Forest Whitaker fits that bill, and he was addressed as such.[8]

The rub is that, despite this display of what some might call genteel racism, Coates admits to wanting to continue his patronage of the deli. He is only awakened to the political reality that he must boycott the store when his wife-partner asks him rhetorically, "What if they did that to your son?" He concludes, "Right then I knew that I was tired of good [white] people, that I had had all the good [white] people I could take."[9]

A similar thought was running through my head when, after I admonished my colleague for his racially insensitive (if not blatantly racist) behavior, he began chronicling all the good things he had done for blacks over his lifespan. When his chronicling of good deeds morphed into a discussion about how his black students at the University of Miami are better filmmakers than his white ones because of their gritty, raw experiences living in the 'hood, I had heard enough. I interrupted his self-aggrandizing, stereotype-riddled meditation and told him that I no longer wished to continue dialoguing with him—that as far as I was concerned the matter was settled. And by settled I meant that I was not about to waste any more of my time, energy, and emotional resources dignifying his apologist gesture. Indeed, my nerves were frayed. His tacit insistence that I hear him out—that I acknowledge that his résumé of antiracist activities qualified him as a good white person despite the fact that he never acknowledged or apologized for his offensive behavior— was far more than I could stomach in that moment. Fortunately, there were still folks waiting to get me to sign copies of their books so I had a convenient excuse to cut the conversation short. I could tell by the expression of determination on his face when he left that our dialogue was not over. A few days later I received an e-mail in the guise of an apology insisting that I misread his intentions and requesting a meeting for lunch. Though I started to ignore the e-mail altogether, I decided, for reasons that I cannot fully understand myself, to answer him. Well, that's not exactly true either. I was, to be frank, disturbed and outraged at the audacity of his white fragility. It was clear to me from the outset that he was operating in a defensive posture borne of a desire to chastise me for disrespecting good white folks, like himself, in my lecture and needing, at the same time, for me to affirm that he was indeed a good white person. His impulse to meet was largely driven, in my estimation, by a desire to "whitesplain" (i.e., defend) rather than own up to his racist behavior. The idea that I somehow "owed" him the opportunity and time to clarify his comments and behavior was itself an outgrowth of white fragility. Again, it never seemed to cross his mind to simply acknowledge the transgression or issue an apology. He was insistent that I was somehow obligated to understand his good intentions and sincerity. So partly out of frustration and partly for my own peace of mind, I delineated my discontent and reiterated that I had no desire to speak on the matter further and certainly no desire to subject myself to more of his parasitical white fragility responses. He reacted to my refusal to meet with an e-mail containing more of the same white fragility logic. But having "said my piece," to invoke another African American colloquialism, I refused to engage any further. In truth, there was nothing more I could add. Besides, the emotional and material stakes in such stressful race-centric engagements are inevitably higher for the historically oppressed group than for the historically oppressive group. Whites are simply defending their right to *remain* socially, culturally, and economically dominant; blacks and people of color are defending their very humanity.

I open this book with this anecdote about my experiences with this liberal white colleague at my 2014 book signing talk in Miami because I want to think critically in *Lovable Racists, Magical Negroes, and White Messiahs* about the emotional tenacity, political utility, and bankability of willful white blindness in the twenty-first century. Indeed, willful white blindness explains, in large part, why spouting racialist language or behaving in a racially insensitive manner does not typically come at a high social or economic cost to whites. One need only be able to offer a perfunctory apology ("My insensitive racial remarks/behavior does not reflect what's in my heart"), plead ignorance ("I now realize that my joke/comment/tweet was offensive and ask that you forgive my insensitivity"), or displace the racist label onto their critics ("I'm not racist for calling young black urban men violent drug pushers; you are for blaming whites for black problems"). A key objective of *Lovable Racists* is to highlight three tropes of white supremacy in lovable racists, white messiahs, and magical negroes that not only help to perpetuate various forms of willful white blindness but also operate as real and symbolic currency in pushing the whitewashed cultural narratives of American exceptionalism, white redemption, self-determination, and racial inclusivity. The trope "lovable racist" reflects the ways in which current iterations of white supremacy have normalized white racist behavior to the point to which only extreme forms of such behavior even register as problematic to most whites. Everyday and institutionalized white supremacy (which informs how whites think about, say, unarmed blacks getting murdered by the police or accounts for the gross inequities in incarceration rates, educational opportunities, and media representation, just to name a few) do not rise to the level of "true" or harmful racist behavior within this mindset. The lovable-racist trope, then, reflects and reifies this paradoxical white supremacist thinking. More specifically, it encourages whites to see racism as a minor character flaw which does not ultimately compromise the moral integrity of the lovable racist. Logistically speaking, the lovable-racist trope requires black/brown complicity in white supremacist ideology to establish cultural legitimacy. That is, lovable racists must convey via black/brown embodied validation that their racism is largely harmless to black/brown folks and people of color in general. This harmless racism is registered through the affection that black/brown folks have toward the lovable racist despite his/her racist mindset. The meteoric rise of Donald Trump to political prominence is a striking case in point. An unapologetic racist and xenophobe, Donald Trump has a small loyal cadre of black and brown folks, including failed GOP presidential candidate–cum–Secretary of Housing and Urban Development Ben Carson, who excuse or justify his racist and xenophobic behavior time and again. Rather than call out this blatant form of racial tokenism, the mainstream white media, including Fox News, CNN, and MSNBC, often give these token black/brown Trump supporters excessive media coverage, obscuring the reality that in his bid for the presidency he polled significantly lower among blacks/brown folks than any GOP presidential candidate in the last quarter-century. This veneer of lovability was further compounded when the iconic comedy show *Saturday Night Live* *(SNL)* featured him as a guest early on in the GOP nomination race following a spate of racist and xenophobic comments, including a wildly inaccurate claim that Mexico was deliberately sending rapists and criminals across the border to the United States. (The reality is that the crime rate among new immigrants, including Mexican immigrants, is significantly *lower* than that of the general population.)[10] Indeed, *SNL* moved forward with hosting

Trump despite receiving intense pressure to drop him from the show from the National Hispanic Leadership (a group comprised of forty Hispanic organizations), the Congressional Hispanic Caucus, and a MoveOn.org campaign that garnered more than 148,000 signatures.[11] Trump rode this media-conspiring brand of lovable racism all the way to the presidency.

The white-messiah trope operates in the service of conflating whiteness with godliness, goodness, spirituality, omnipotence, purity, and universality. The tenacity of this trope is reflected in the perpetual and even violent resistance by whites to allowing omnipotent figures, like the Judeo-Christian savior figure Jesus Christ or even godlike mythical figures like Santa Claus, to be represented racially as anything other than white. Further, the white-messiah trope depends parasitically on seeing blacks as perpetually in need of white guidance, love, understanding, forgiveness, mercy, inspiration, intellect, and/or financial assistance. Like the lovable-racist trope, the white-messiah trope also depends on a level of black/brown complicity in white oppression to sustain itself. This pattern is on display in all facets of our culture, from how Hollywood perpetuates and sells white-redemption and white-messiah scripts (think *Avatar*, *The Green Mile*, *The Help*, and *McFarland, USA*) to how the National Football League, the most popular and lucrative professional sports franchise in the United States, brands its star players (i.e, white stars like Tom Brady and Peyton Manning are cerebral, posed, decisive, commanding, and heroic; black stars like Russell Wilson and Cam Newton are athletic, strong, dynamic, elusive, and cocky).

The magical-negro trope serves a largely complementary role to both the lovable-racist trope and the white-messiah trope as it situates blacks as mascots, inspirations, and/or surrogates for the celebration or affirmation of white humanity. The magical negro tends to be self-sacrificial to a pathological extent, existing almost exclusively to usher whites through emotional, social, or economic crises. This trope is also on display in how the history of black struggle is represented in the educational system and beyond. Radical black human rights movements and black leaders who inspired them become deradicalized to the point of gross historical distortion. Their laudable stories of resistance, organizing, strategizing, and outwitting their white oppressors in pursuit of racial equality and social justice are transformed politically via this trope into feel-good narratives about the American Dream, white redemption, and American exceptionalism. By extension, black antislavery revolutionaries and Civil Rights activists emerge in our national history as mascots of an underdog democracy. Indeed, the magical-negro trope explains how the political right (whose attacks on President Barack Obama have been transparently racist and xenophobic in nature) has been able to construe his election and reelection as the country's first black president as proof that we have become postracial as a nation and thus no longer need the political safeguards like the 1965 Voting Rights Act (which has been subsequently weakened by the conservative-leaning Supreme Court)[12] to protect the civil rights of blacks and people of color.

The wicked irony is that President Obama strategically employed the magical-negro trope during both his successful presidential campaigns to assuage white fears that a black president would challenge or upset the status quo dominance of white power. He ran, on the one hand, as a presidential candidate who *happened* to be black and, on the other hand, as a candidate whose blackness and multiracial*ness* allowed him to appreciate the plights of blacks and people of color. More specifically, he employed his experiences as a mixed-race, multicultural kid from Hawaii who was raised by his white mother and grandparents and abandoned by his black Kenyan father as a way to both identify with and separate himself from the "black experience" in the United States and the legacy of racial discrimination. Adherence to white values catapulted him to success. Working as a community organizer in poor black communities in Chicago helped him empathize with the plight of blacks and Latinos. He strategically embodied the possibilities of the (white) American dream with his rags to riches spiel while relating enough to blacks and people of color on a symbolic level (like listening to hip hop music and giving fist bumps to his outspoken, smart, and derrière-blessed black wife, Michelle) to appear to be a cultural insider. He was a Harvard-educated, Jay Z–listening, black woman–loving model minority with swag.

However brilliant this employment of the magical-negro trope was as a campaign strategy to quell liberal white fears and recruit voters of color, it was hardly significant in terms of altering white views of black humanity. As the magical-negro trope is designed to erase blacks' complex humanity, authenticate white paternalism, and explain away, if not justify, white domination, the election and reelection of President Obama confirmed for many whites across political affiliations that racism was not only passé but that whites were the chief targets of discrimination. Tellingly, the dominant racial narrative about Obama's election and reelection continues to be that the white vote is what twice catapulted him to the White House. The reality, however, is that whites voted overwhelmingly for the white candidate in *both* elections.[13] It was, in fact, the African American and Latino vote that carried the day for Obama in both campaigns but most saliently in 2012 when Obama lost significant ground to Mitt Romney among white voters and white women in particular, whose vote was split 56% for Romney and only 42% for Obama.[14] As history shows time and again, invented racial realities that reinforce white supremacy have enormous cultural capital and routinely "trumps" the historical record.

To elucidate the tenacity of these white supremacist racial tropes in public and private spaces, *Lovable Racists, Magical Negroes, and White Messiahs* considers the extent to which willful white blindness—past and present—informs the low bar of expectations that blacks have toward whites in the twenty-first century when it comes to empathy with their plight. From slavery to the present, blacks have been compelled to rely, if not manipulated into relying, on so-called white goodwill and charity for independence, freedom, and financial stability. The aforementioned colloquialism "good white folks," which was in vogue during the post-Reconstruction era, grows out of this thinking. Then as now, the "goodness" of good white folks was measured against status quo white hostility, violence, and socioeconomic oppression. The metaphoric bar of black expectation of humane treatment from whites was often set very low, meaning that blacks experienced white common decency, to borrow Bennett's terminology, as laudable and even heroic. This calculus of low expectation, gratitude, and indebtedness made blacks who pushed for true racial equality seem radical and dangerous to whites and to a significant number of blacks.

James Baldwin and Toni Morrison come immediately to mind as artists-activists who have introduced critical models to think through such complex issues, especially as they inform black consciousness and self-determination. An often-overlooked trailblazer in whiteness studies, Baldwin treats race in general as a failed social construction and white supremacy in particular as a pathological discourse with dire ideological, social, and psychological consequences for even the whites who invented and policed it. Baldwin argued that whites could only enjoy their privilege fully on an emotional level if they convinced themselves that blacks were somehow less human than whites and deserving of domination. To emotionally substantiate this narrative of white supremacy/black inferiority, whites also needed to manufacture the approval and, in some cases, the forgiveness of African Americans. In *The Fire Next Time* Baldwin embodies his politic by invoking the parasitical relationship between black servants and white employers in the pre–Civil Rights era and demonstrating how willful white blindness operates to appease white guilt and reinforces the racial status quo of power. Using the white claim that black servants frequently steal from their white employers as a political touchstone, Baldwin avers that black servants "have been smuggling odds and ends out of white homes for generations . . . and white people have been *delighted* to have them do it . . . because it has assuaged a dim guilt and testified to the intrinsic superiority of white people."[15] Baldwin identifies the ways that severe economic exploitation of black labor pressed some blacks to steal from their white employers as a means of survival. Ideologically speaking, whites were "delighted" by these acts of survival because they confirmed the discourse of white superiority/black inferiority upon which racial disparities of power are premised. White discrimination toward and mistreatment of black servants were not the problem; thieving black servants were. Wedded as they were to images of themselves as fair, just, and generous, whites could dismiss black discontent as bogus and use such incidents of theft to justify mistrusting and exploiting blacks. Because of such widespread economic and physical white exploitation, whites who treated black domestics with a modicum of decency and respect or paid them slightly better than the deplorable racial salary standards of the era were perceived as good white folks. Rather than challenge twisted white notions of white goodness, this low bar of black expectation served indirectly to reinforce it.

Like Baldwin before her, Morrison understood intuitively that white identity was parasitically and inextricably tied to black identity. Encouraged ideologically to see blacks rather than whites as raced beings, Morrison had difficulty as both a writer and a literary critic understanding how white-authored literary texts, especially those written between the post-Reconstruction and the Civil Rights eras, could be so devoid of the black presence despite the centrality of blacks to white society and consciousness. When she began to flip the racial script and consider whites' intense investment in racial discourse and how that investment flies under the radar of critical scrutiny within and beyond the academy, she realized that she had been asking the wrong question; that the conspicuous black absence and parasitical black/white relations in white texts reflected a crisis of white identity and superiority. She argued that what whites revealed about blacks in their texts was self-reflective; it clued the reader into the intellectual and emotional jiu-jitsu required to erase or distort the complexity of African/African American humanity.

Recalling Baldwin's servant/employer analogy, Morrison hones in on the servant/master relationship between Till and Sapphira in Willa Cather's *Sapphira and the Slave Girl* to illustrate how willful white blindness plays out ideologically and materially. What she ultimately conveys is that even in a novel that has an overt antislavery message, the unstated rules of white hegemony mean that the complex humanity of the black characters and the black women characters in particular cannot be fully acknowledged or rendered. Liberation as such must be imagined by and rendered though white consciousness, meaning that the black characters are perpetually indebted to whites *even* for conceptualizing a path beyond the very institution of slavery that whites have imposed onto them. For this racial calculus to work, willful white blindness and black humanity must remain underground and unnamed. Morrison argues that this racial calculus explains why Cather titled the novel *Sapphira and the Slave Girl* rather than *Sapphira and Nancy*. Registering the slave girl Nancy's humanity on the same level as the white protagonist Sapphira would have required Cather to confront the unspeakable racial apparatus that normativizes white supremacy/black inferiority. Condemning slavery as the novel does is not the same as rejecting the discourse of white supremacy. As humanity is raced white within a white hegemonic society, the truly revolutionary move would have been to attack the discourse of white supremacy that era(c)es the humanity of enslaved blacks: "To have called the book 'Sapphira and Nancy' would have lured Cather into dangerous deep water. Such a title would have clarified and drawn attention immediately to what the novel obscures even as it makes a valiant effort at honest engagement: the sycophancy of white identity."[16]

As Morrison points out time and again, the actions and behavior of the black mother figure Till defies logic; she sits idly by as her white mistress, Sapphira, schemes to have Till's only daughter, Nancy, raped in a twisted plot to regain the affections of her husband. Cather's skewed portraits of Till and Nancy, then, reveal nothing of substance about black women's consciousness or human complexity. Rather they expose the "interdependent workings of power, race, and sexuality in a white woman's battle for coherence."[17]

I find it instructive that Morrison chooses to critique a white text that "makes a valiant effort at honest engagement" to make a point about the "sycophancy of white identity." Morrison's message is that "honesty" does not let Cather or whites off the hook for perpetuating and policing white supremacy. What Morrison is calling an "honest engagement" with racial matters, Baldwin refers to sardonically in *The Fire Next Time* as "white innocence." White innocence is another way to characterize willful white blindness. Whites often genuinely do not see the consequences of their oppression or privilege because they have conditioned themselves not to see them. Baldwin encapsulates this paradox, writing, "It is the innocence which constitutes the crime."[18]

Here the inextricable relationship between willful white blindness and blacks' dangerously low expectation of white empathy/insight on race matters becomes more evident. It is rare indeed—even in this day and time—to get most whites to acknowledge that racism still exists or, for that matter, that slavery, segregation, and racial terrorism of the past are responsible in large part for the problems that plague Black America in the twenty-first century. (I cannot count how many times I have heard whites—liberal and conservative—invoke the election of the first black president to discount or minimize black claims of racial inequality in this historical moment.) Baldwin's letter to his nephew which opens *The Fire Next Time*, and from which the "white innocence" comment originates, is highly attentive to this phenomena of willful white blindness and denial. Baldwin is acutely aware, for instance, that blacks are conditioned to feel indebted to whites on a number of emotional, social, and economic levels. He tells his nephew, who is named after him, that the

details and symbols of your life have been deliberately constructed to make you believe what white people say about you. Please try to remember that what they believe, as well as what they do and cause you to endure, does not testify to your inferiority but to their inhumanity and fear. Please try to be clear, dear James, through the storm which rages about your youthful head today, about the reality which lies behind the words *acceptance* and *integration*. There is no reason for you to try to become like white people and there is no basis whatever for their impertinent assumption that *they* must accept *you*. The really terrible thing, old buddy, is that *you* must accept *them*.[19]

The idea of indebtedness to whites derives from the thinking that whites must "accept" blacks into US society and make the grand sacrifice of tolerating their integration in white schools and other previously segregated spaces. Violently and systematically denying human rights to African Americans emerges as a necessary evil of Western civilization. Within this white mindset, then, slavery and segregation are read as a small price for Africans to have paid to become civilized and reap the spoils of Western culture. If slavery and segregation were harsh, they were still a far cry from the savagery and primitivism of Africa. This idea of being indebted to whites—which, of course, drives willful white blindness—radically informs black notions of self-determination and agency. Even if the reality is that black activism and the threat of large-scale black rebellion played a significant role in forcing whites to end slavery and then later segregation, the dominant white narrative—reinforced in the media, politics, popular culture, and academics—says that white goodwill combined with American exceptionalism were the chief catalysts for change.

Baldwin was trying to expose the lie of this thinking in the 1960s to prepare his nephew for the ideological, social, and economic assault of white supremacy. Moreover, he was trying to get his nephew to see that whites were the ones indebted on multiple levels to blacks; that their claims to the contrary were a smokescreen to appease their guilty conscience and to justify the maintenance of racial inequities beyond slavery.

Baldwin's mindset is important emotionally because blacks—then and now—are encouraged socially to celebrate and/or reward even the most minimal gesture of white empathy. The black community's long-time love affair with white messiahs Bill Clinton is a striking case in point. Culturally speaking, white-messiah figures like Clinton are able to leverage blacks' historically low expectation of just white treatment to appear heroic in their empathy toward black concerns. Because whites of Clinton's ilk, including his wife and former Democratic presidential candidate Hillary Clinton, get so much black love for so little white sacrifice, they experience themselves as exceptionally liberal and antiracist. Bill Clinton's track record in terms of helping black communities during his two terms in office is uneven at best. For example, even as the overall economy improved and upper-crust blacks experienced higher earnings, the black poor took a beating under his administration's welfare reform and the wealth gap between whites and blacks continued to grow. And though he has since admitted to not doing enough in office to eliminate the deplorable sentencing disparities in drug offenses between powdered cocaine (the drug of choice in the white middle class) and crack cocaine (the default choice for poor black and brown communities that can't afford the powdered stuff), the crime bills that he did manage to pass fueled the prison industrial complex and further exacerbated the situation of incarceration for black men. Yet despite this atrocious record, blacks remained his most loyal constituency. Indeed, he enjoyed high approval ratings in black spaces even during the height of the Monica Lewinsky scandal and the subsequent impeachment proceedings. The truth of the matter is that it was Clinton's high comfort level with blacks, not his policies, which set him apart from all the previous presidents and endeared him to Black America. Toni Morrison encapsulated this sentiment when she quipped during the impeachment proceedings that he was the first black president. So accustomed to being treated as second-class citizens and having to fight tooth and nail for progress even under supposedly black-friendly administrations, many blacks viewed Clinton—with his visible comfort level with black folks and his high cultural IQ—as unique and laudatory. His comfort level with blacks combined with blacks' low expectation of white empathy allowed Clinton to appear like a champion of black folks when in reality his welfare reform and crime policies have had a devastating impact on black communities. Blacks were so enamored of Clinton, in fact, that many incorrectly believed that blacks were doing better than whites economically during his presidency.[20] As Melissa Harris-Perry reports, "There is no evidence to suggest that African Americans were in a better economic position than whites at any time in American history, including during Clinton's presidency."[21] The bar of racial empathy was set so low for Clinton that it was easy for him to lull many blacks into a "perceptual fog" with his "hypnotic racial dance of cultural authenticity."[22]

Hillary Clinton has learned how to work the white-messiah angle to great effect as well. During the earlier stages of her second presidential campaign when the Black Lives Matter (BLM) movement was still gaining political momentum she refused to embrace the term "Black Lives Matter" for fear of offending white independents and her white Democratic base. When asked during press conferences and televised interviews how she thought about the term "black lives matter" she would routinely respond that "all lives matter." When her chief Democrat presidential rival, Bernie Sanders, became a target of the movement and began receiving bad press as a result, Clinton—who desperately needed the black vote in order to win the White House—switched positions. Not only did she begin to embrace the term, she met with BLM leaders on multiple occasions and aggressively courted their endorsement. She also began openly impugning her GOP presidential rivals and especially Donald Trump for their refusal to follow her example as if critical reflection and respect for diversity, not social pressure and political expediency, sparked her "change of heart." Even though positioning herself as a white messiah against Trump didn't ultimately generate enough black turnout to overcome Trump's white voter surge in key rustbelt states, she did win 88% of the black vote. Indeed, had she performed as well as Obama did among white rural voters in 2012 (he received 48% support compared to Clinton's 34% support) her 88% win margin among black voters might have been enough to have won the presidency. It bears mentioning that Clinton won the popular vote by almost 3 million votes—the largest margin of victory by far of any candidate in history that has lost the Electoral College vote. It also bears mentioning that in 1787 the Electoral College was designed via legislative compromise to allow wealthy white male slaveowners in the South to count three-fifths of their slaves as votes. Given this historical racial reality, it is all the more troubling that a rich white male candidate running on a thinly veiled white supremacist patriarchal platform lost the popular vote by such a wide margin (comprising a disproportionate majority of people of color and especially African Americans) but still won the Electoral College vote and by default the presidency. Essentially, an outmoded and undeniably racist voting system that was devised well over two hundred years ago is still bearing fruit in the twenty-first century for wealthy white men, like Trump, who routinely and unapologetically exploit their intersecting race, gender, and class privilege. The voting system is rigged indeed but *not* in favor of true democracy.

Lovable Racists, Magical Negroes, and White Messiahs grows out of my frustration with the tenacity of such white supremacist tropes and how effective they continue to be at devaluing black lives and trivializing black oppression. I am acutely attentive to the relationship between willful white blindness and blacks' low expectation of white empathy and fairness because of the effect that it had on my thinking as a child and the effect that I see it having on my own children. While as a nation we have certainly progressed on many racial matters over my short lifetime (in large part because of the fearless efforts of black activists and everyday folks willing to lay down their lives for freedom and equality), I am compelled to agree with Derrick Bell's assertion in *Silent Covenant* that "racism is permanent in this country."[23] Pessimistic though he may seem at first blush, Bell speaks to the tenacity of white supremacist ideology in our republic. How else does one explain how we shifted as a country from electing the first black president to two terms to electing a rich white unapologetic bigot and xenophobe with a nasty, if not pathological, habit of lying to the American public and reinforcing vile stereotypes about African Americans and people of color? To this political end, it is important to interrogate willful white blindness and attendant master narratives of white redemption because one who controls the master narrative controls the perception of reality or, at the very least, dictates what the republic legitimizes, perpetuates, and polices as reality.

Edward Said underscores the dangers of this phenomenon of framing cultural realities in his explication of why in 1798 French military leader Napoleon Bonaparte brought a small army of scholars with him during his military conquest of Egypt. Imperialist that he was, Napoleon was well aware that in order to colonize Egypt, he needed to dominant them militarily *and* ideologically. The latter required rewriting their history, culture, and religion (which he did using his imported orientalist scholars along with local imams, cadis, muftis, and ulemas that he recruited and coerced to do his bidding) to link European culture/society to the dawn of civilization and intellectual superiority, erstwhile relegating Egyptian culture and Islam to primitive status.

By taking Egypt, then, a modern power would naturally demonstrate its strength and justify history; Egypt's own destiny was to be annexed, to Europe preferably. In addition, this power would also enter a history whose common element was defined by figures no less great than Homer, Alexander, Caesar, Plato, Solon, and Pythagoras, who graced the Orient with their prior present there. The Orient, in short, existed as a set of values attached, not to its modern realities, but to a series of valorized contacts it had had with a distant European past.[24]

Napoleon was able to perpetuate a historical falsehood—that the Orient and the world at large was indebted to European culture for the whole of civilization in the modern era—and leverage that falsehood economically, militarily, and socially to impose its will on the Orient. One needn't be a scholar of the first order to connect the dots between what Said is explaining about Napoleon and orientalism to what is happening politically and racially in places like Texas and Arizona in terms of rewriting the historic record to explain away and/or justify white dominance and literally outlaw counter-hegemonic discourses such as Mexican American Studies. In a wickedly perverse and seductive way conservative state legislators in both states have turned the tables on those who would seek to hold the United States accountable for its history of human trafficking, slavery, and imperialist conquest. Critical engagements with our nation's troubled and troubling past are treated as unpatriotic, socially disruptive, and bordering on treason. Schools, administrators, and teachers who have bucked the state dictates have been made an example of via firings, pulling of school funding, and the like. What's scary about these recent developments is that it hasn't sparked a major outcry from the mainstream. If anything, many conservative governors from states like Florida and Wisconsin see Texas and Arizona as trailblazers and make no bones about wanting to follow their lead. The proof, as they say, is in the pudding. The defunding and/or outright elimination of African American, Mexican, and women-studies programs in higher education is accelerating with a vengeance across the country.

Lovable Racists, Magical Negroes, and White Messiahs seeks, above all, to sound the alarm about the seemingly innocuous tropes and narratives of white redemption that abound in our society and that engender the notion that blacks are perpetually indebted to whites for liberating, civilizing, and enlightening them. Focusing on the presence of these racial tropes and narratives in various mediums, ranging from novels to films to newscasting and political campaigns, this book considers the making and unmaking of racial realities and the political stakes therein for African Americans. It also considers how to hold whites accountable for their willful white blindness and rally blacks to push back against such tropes and narratives that continue to render black pathology and white supremacy normative.

ONE

Good Slave Masters Don't Exist: Lovable Racists and the Crisis of Authorship in *Twelve Years a Slave*

The treatment of enslaved Africans varied. *Some slaves reported that their masters treated them kindly.* To protect their investment, some slaveholders provided adequate food and clothing for their slaves. PASSAGE FROM A SEVENTH-GRADE HISTORY BOOK IN TEXAS

Ghostwritten by David Wilson, a white attorney and aspiring novelist, Solomon Northup's slave narrative, *Twelve Years a Slave*, abounds with shady white characters, including slavers, who receive disturbingly flattering and even heroic treatment. The most revealing in this regard is Solomon's description of his first master, William Ford, at the outset of chapter 7; a description which is conspicuously juxtaposed to a heart-wrenching scene at the end of chapter 6 of a slave woman, Eliza, being torn from her daughter during a slave auction. From a writerly perspective, to borrow Toni Morrison's coinage, the juxtaposition of these scenes exposes a curious anxiety about painting all white slave owners as complicit in human trafficking, dehumanization, labor exploitation, and religious terrorism. As the reader will recall, Eliza was coerced into concubinage by her former master, now deceased, and, consequently, gave birth to two of his children, a boy and girl. Eliza's son had just been sold off when this scene occurs. In utter desperation, Eliza pleads with Ford, who has just made an offer for her, to also purchase her daughter. Ford relents and offers to buy her daughter at a "reasonable price." The auctioneer-owner Theophilus Freeman, whom Solomon describes as a cold-blooded monster of a man, refuses to sell her, noting that her Eurocentric features make her a highly lucrative commodity; the implication being that he can groom and eventually sell her as a high-end concubine to wealthy white men. The chapter ends with a diatribe on Eliza's agony over her forced separation from her children.

Chapter 7 opens with a rather inexplicable homage to Ford and good slave masters. Indeed the shift in tone and message startles the reader:

In many northern minds, perhaps, the idea of a man holding his brother man in servitude, and the traffic in human flesh, may seem altogether incompatible with their conceptions of a moral or religious life. From descriptions of such men as . . . Freeman, and others hereinafter mentioned, they are led to despise and execrate the whole class of slaveholders, indiscriminately. But I was sometime his slave, and had an opportunity of learning well his character and disposition, and it is but simple justice to him when I say, in my opinion, there never was a more kind, noble, candid, Christian man than William Ford. The influences and associations that had always surrounded him, blinded him to the inherent wrong at the bottom of the system of Slavery. He never doubted the moral right of one man holding another in subjection. Looking through the same medium with his fathers before him, he saw things in the same light. Brought up under other circumstances and other influences, his notions would undoubtedly have been different. *Nevertheless, he was a model master, walking uprightly, according to the light of his understanding, and fortunate was the slave who came to his possession. Were all men such as he, Slavery would be deprived of more than half its bitterness.*[1]

Though Ford is no less complicit and accountable than Freeman for participating in the enslavement and dehumanization of blacks, Solomon makes a clear and indeed dramatic distinction between the two men. To wit, Solomon experiences Freeman as inhumane and cruel because he has no conscience about separating mothers from their children or grooming children to be concubines and prostitutes. In contrast, Solomon experiences Ford as kindhearted and fair because Ford has the emotional wherewithal to empathize with Eliza's suffering as a mother to the point of attempting to purchase her daughter. Of course, in order for us to embrace Solomon's perspective we have to accept that Ford, a shrewd businessman whose wealth depends largely on slave labor, is oblivious to the market value of Eliza's biracial daughter. Moreover, we must ignore the fact that Ford's purchasing of Eliza is what precipitates the separation of mother from child. Granted, the separation of mother and child may ultimately have been inevitable given the circumstances, but Ford's participation therein was certainly not.

Indicative of many scholars who engage with white supremacist ideology in *Twelve Years*, Tara T. Green argues that Solomon's flattering portrait of good slave masters is strategic. Solomon makes sure to separate the sin of slavery from the white sinners in slaveholders because he does not want to alienate his mostly white abolitionist-minded audience. That is, he "avoid[s] placing all white people into the category of the wicked" because he is acutely aware that even his politically sympathetic white readership has deep investments in white supremacist ideology and seeing whites generally (including slaveholders) as innately well-intentioned and with morals. Green references Frederick Douglass's 1845 *Narrative*—wherein he makes distinctions among whites in terms of their (mis)treatment of slaves[2]—to identify, contextualize, and defend Solomon's tactic of appeasing whites. Crucially overlooked in this comparison is the extent to which Douglass interrogated and repudiated the notion of "good slave masters" in the *Narrative*. He is most insulted by Mr. Auld's gesture of giving him a small portion of his earned wages back to him. Rather than view such a gesture as laudable (because most slave masters were not willing to compensate the enslaved even a little), Douglass sees it as a wicked and pathological tactic that allowed Mr. Auld to assuage his guilt for enslaving and robbing him. Indeed, Douglass deciphers the apparatus of complicity in oppression upon which the white supremacist system of slavery is premised. Brilliant strategist that he is, Douglass accepts the insufficient bribes, manipulates Mr. Auld into trusting him, and then eventually escapes to freedom.

It is thus deeply problematic, if not shortsighted, to compare *Twelve Years* to the *Narrative* because Solomon Northup did not have the authorial control or political agency that Frederick Douglass possessed. While it is certainly plausible that Northup's flattering portraits of good white slave masters as rendered through his white ghostwriter, David Wilson, was a strategy rather than a true reflection of his feelings toward whites, it is equally, if not more, plausible that the filter of white authorship and editorial privilege altered or even undermined Northup's interrogation of white supremacist slavery in the text. Even from what little we know about Wilson, there is ample reason to believe that he took great liberties with Solomon's story. As Solomon Northup's biographer, Sue Eakin, explains, Wilson was infatuated with the popularity and financial success of Harriet Beecher Stowe's *Uncle Tom's Cabin*. She opines that the uncanny resemblances between characters in both texts reveal Wilson's desire to reproduce the global prestige and financial success of Stowe's *Uncle*, a text that condemns the practice of slavery even as it reifies the basic tenets of white supremacy. Did Wilson's desire to recreate the financial and political success of *Uncle* prompt him to take liberties with Solomon's accounts of slavery, especially in regards to the treatment of white supremacy and Christianity? The heightened and violent state of white surveillance during the antebellum era (even among antislavery whites) makes it is difficult to fathom that Solomon was free to interrogate the white supremacist underpinnings of chattel slavery. Even if we conclude *Twelve Years* accurately reflects Solomon's perspectives on Ford and "good masters," we are still left to ponder to what extent his perspectives were a consequence of blacks' forced reliance on white sponsorship for authorial legitimacy, social justice, and physical protection. Did Solomon's feelings of obligation to his white sponsor, Henry Northup, inform how he engaged white supremacy in *Twelve Years*, including the use of Christianity to manipulate, pacify, and terrorize the enslaved? To what degree did Solomon's undeniable investment in white supremacy—conscious and unconscious—obscure his perspective about good slave masters?

Alas, these are questions that will likely remain unanswered because only scant information exists about the lives of Solomon Northup, Henry Northup, and David Wilson. That said, even if we were somehow able to retrieve historical documentation that could settle the question of whether David Wilson took political and creative liberties with Solomon Northup's story, such knowledge would provide only limited insights into why an abolitionist text would offer such competing notions of white slaveholding culture; why it would sympathize with rather than obliterate the southern romance of lovable slave masters and contented slaves.

Departing sharply from conventional readings of *Twelve Years*, I will engage Solomon's flattering rendering of good white slave masters and his curiously stereotypical and, at times, unsympathetic rendering of black women as a problem of white supremacist ideology rather than as a subversive tactic to critique it without alienating white readers. Indeed, this chapter will treat Solomon's conspicuous blind spots regarding manipulative, paternalistic slavers such as Ford as a result of what I call "lovable-racist thinking." A lovable racist is a white character who is rendered in such a way that it encourages the reader or viewer to see his/her racism or inhumanity toward blacks or people of color as a minor, if not justifiable, character flaw. In order for lovable racists to escape serious scrutiny as racists, they must be validated in some way morally, ethically, or socially as "good people" by the very group that they exploit and/or discriminate against. Within this lovable-racist calculus, the validating black/brown character is also elevated to hero status by virtue of his/her ability to see the lovable racist's redeeming qualities beyond their racist behavior. As readers/viewers we are often seduced into identifying and empathizing with lovable racists because they are typically chief protagonist(s) and thus the most developed and sympathetically rendered character(s) in novels, nonfiction texts, television series, and films. Indeed, it is highly unlikely that anyone would read Mark Twain's *Adventures of Huckleberry Finn* and identify more with nigger Jim than with Huck Finn. Or that anyone would watch the film "Gran Torino" and identify with the gangbanger set, over the gun-toting, xenophobe, and racist Walt Kowalski. The reason for this is that the novel and film render the racialist white characters in such a way as to endear them to us—though Huck Finn is a sadistic and cruel man-child who delights in torturing Jim, he ultimately winds up appearing caring and humane toward Jim. Walt Kowalski wins our collective hearts with his conventional patriarchal fathering of Hmong teenagers Thao and Sue, which includes sacrificing life and limb to protect them from black and brown gangbangers. This political calculus amplifies the humanity of the white racist characters while erasing, or rendering trivial, the humanity of the raced other(s). In fact, this is done with such great effect in "Gran Torino" that Walt emerges as a white messiah/Christ figure as well as a lovable racist. Because the film treats the gangbangers as heartless thugs, ignoring not only their humanity but also the white supremacist capitalism that has decimated their community, the viewers cheer when they get their comeuppance and lionize Walt for his messianic self-sacrifice.

The open secret of American history is that until recently—say, the last fifty years—black experiences of white domination have been largely erased or distorted to the point of romance. What this phenomenon has meant—and means—is that the black creative enterprise, including writing, theater, film, and music, has taken on greater significance in the contemporary moment in terms of correcting this white historical erasure.[3] Logistically speaking, the reader should keep in mind that when I refer to Solomon as the author of *Twelve Years* heretofore, I am doing so with an understanding that Solomon's experiences are being filtered through the perspective of a white man in David Wilson, who was most likely free to embellish/alter the slave narrative as he saw fit. If, racially speaking, Wilson was like the overwhelming majority of whites of his day (including many abolitionists), then sustaining white supremacy was not incompatible with wanting to end slavery. After all, slavery was economically disadvantageous to working-class whites—the bulk of society—because it suppressed the value of white labor. While the cultural capital of dominating blacks ultimately trumped these disadvantages for most southern working-class whites, it was a key bone of contention for many northern whites, meaning that the motivation to abolish slavery for many whites was driven by self-interest and economics, not a desire for racial equality and social justice. If indeed Wilson did take political liberties with Solomon's story, these sociohistorical phenomena provide possible motives why, as a northern white,[4] he would do so. If, alas, the text accurately represents Solomon's mindset, then it exposes more about the deleterious consequences of internalized white supremacy and white supremacist terrorism on black consciousness than it enlightens us about the racial realities of slavery.

Lovable-Racist Thinking and the Erasure of Black Subjectivity

To, at once, identify the tenacity of lovable-racist thinking (especially in the post–Civil Rights era) and the potential to expose and explode it in the twenty-first century, this chapter will put *Twelve Years* in critical dialogue with the latest film adaptation, "12 Years A Slave."[5] More pointedly, this chapter argues that "12 Years" operates politically to "correct" the lovable racists' (mis)representations of black humanity and white goodwill. To be clear, what is being corrected is not the historical record per se, but rather Solomon's warped white supremacist/apologist perspective on white culpability, paternalism, and religious practice. Attentive to the serious limitations of Solomon's racial insights in the slave narrative, the film"-12 Years" refocuses on Solomon's social and ideological conditioning" as a black subject in a pathologically white supremacist society—a move which allows us to see why an otherwise self-actualized man would romanticize white paternalism and become a policing agent therein. What this move also throws radically into focus is that celebrated white paternalists, like Mr. and Mrs. Ford in the slave narrative, are, in fact, willfully blind agents of human atrocities or what I am calling lovable racists. The key corrective intervention here is that refocusing on Solomon's racial conditioning allows us to see the complexity of black humanity in the ways that Solomon and other blacks cope with and negotiate hyper white surveillance, racial terrorism, and legalized dehumanization. Unlike the slave narrative which privileges

Solomon's perspective and complicity within the lovable-racist calculus, the film includes the critical perspectives of other enslaved blacks and clears a space therein to interrogate the problems of lovable-racist thinking.

That the key voices of interrogation in the film happen to come from black women (who, with few notable exceptions, are cast in the slave narrative as weak and unsophisticated)[6] is hardly an accident. Screenwriter John Ridley, in collaboration with director Steve McQueen, takes a decidedly intersectional approach to refocusing the critical gaze as it concerns lovable racists and white supremacist pathology in the slave narrative. That is, Ridley attends to unique intersectional race, gender, and class dynamics of the experience of the enslaved so that we can see that Solomon's insights about how to negotiate slavery are not necessarily representative or inclusive of all blacks, especially black women. Indeed, the film employs black women to critique white male supremacist pathology in all its various iterations, including how it implicates white women (like Mrs. Ford and Mrs. Epps), and enslaved black men, like Solomon, in the erasure of black women's unique status as both victims and agents of rebellion. Concomitantly, Eliza emerges as a key mouthpiece for interrogating Solomon's romanticized view of Ford as a "good master" and what I call his "double consciousness survivalist thinking" and symptoms of "battered slave syndrome." Invoking W. E. B. Du Bois's theory, the term double consciousness survivalist thinking reflects a mindset of fear, anxiety, and accommodationism driven largely by hyper white surveillance, terrorism, and group-oriented violence. I use the term battered slave syndrome, which recalls the term "battered wife syndrome," to clear a space to think about Solomon's blindness toward paternalist whites, like the Fords, as symptomatic of his violent physical and psychological conditioning under slavery. Indeed, I want to register how the violent and paternalist relationship between slave and master, which is ostensibly structured upon a white patriarchal model in which the enslaved (across gender lines) are feminized and infantilized, informs Solomon's investment in white paternalism and, by turns, his unwillingness to escape by himself or with the help of other slaves. A key symptom of battered wife syndrome is the conditioned belief, borne of fear and violent verbal and physical assault, that you cannot escape the abusive relationship; that compromising with your abuser on his terms, and with the misguided belief that things will get better over time, is the best way to manage the relationship. Ridley's decision to expose Solomon's double consciousness survivalist mindset and battered slave syndrome behavior via Eliza (who is represented in the slave narrative as being without agency or political consciousness) is crucial, considering the tendency within black spaces, from slave narratives to current discourses of black struggle, to radically downplay or erase the intersectional complexities of victimization and personal/political agency. It is also through the women characters in the film—namely Eliza and Patsey—that white women's conspiracy with white men in slavery is thrown brilliantly into focus. This is an important intervention considering that white women's agency as co-conspirators in oppression with white men receives relatively little critical attention in discussions of slave culture.

Before delving into how the film operates as a corrective apparatus, it is important to establish how the slave narrative reifies and even polices lovable-racist thinking (including its celebration of Victorian white womanhood and concomitant erasure of black women's unique subjectivity as enslaved women) via Solomon's narration. The most consequential lovable-racist character in the slave narrative is Mr. Ford. Time and again throughout the narrative Solomon intervenes to distinguish Mr. Ford's brand of slavery from the other white slave owners. Most troubling about this intervention is the extent to which it encourages the reader to view as redemptive the pathological practice of grooming slaves to embrace whites' inhumanity and exploitation. What Solomon experiences as humane, if not heroic, treatment from Ford is simply a more sophisticated form of human exploitation premised on grooming emotional complicity rather than terrorizing/beating the enslaved into compliance. Indeed, like a seasoned sexual predator, Ford grooms Solomon and his slaves to see him as set apart morally and religiously from their other predator-slavers because he *allows* them to read the Bible (which is against the law) and registers their humanity when it is advantageous for him to do so (as when he sides with Solomon over white foreman Adam Taydem regarding building the transporter-raft). Ford's strategy of using religion to control and manipulate the enslaved recalls Frederick Douglass's discussion of white men and slave religion in *The Narrative*. Douglass wails against such masters, going so far as to argue that he preferred atheist masters to religious ones because antebellum Christianity empowered white supremacy and provided white masters with additional emotional capital to justify their domination/exploitation of enslaved Africans. Morrison offers a more pointed critique in *Beloved* in her characterization of Mr. Garner, who referred to his enslaved males as "men" and even allowed them to carry firearms. As Paul D's crisis of masculinity reveals throughout the novel, Mr. Garner's provisional extension of humanity toward the enslaved served only to bolster his feeling of superiority (including over other slave owners) and cultivate loyalty and admiration from the enslaved. Groomed to see Mr. Garner as a type of white messiah who dictated the terms of his humanity and manhood, Paul D struggles mightily with feelings of inadequacy as a man after Mr. Garner dies and schoolteacher takes control over the plantation and strips them of their (falsely) perceived masculine agency, including carrying firearms. As I have noted elsewhere, these gendered feelings of inadequacy carry over to Paul D's postslavery life and nearly sabotage his relationship with Sethe.[7]

Close inspection reveals that Mr. Ford embodies a version of Mr. Garner's warped ego and slave strategy. The problem is that Solomon confuses Mr. Ford's grooming and self-serving imperatives as heroic expressions of kindness and (Christian) love in the face of white inhumanity. Consider Solomon's reaction of deep gratitude to Ford after he intervenes to "defend" Solomon against Tibeats. Referring to Solomon alternately as a "good boy" and a "good nigger" (to which Solomon takes no issue), Ford admonishes Tibeats within earshot of Solomon, whom he has tried to lynch, for being a cruel master and mishandling of his charges. Ford tells Tibeats that resorting to violence and murder is not a productive way of dealing with slaves; that doing so "will have a pernicious influence, and set them running away" to hide in the swamps. He further avers, "A little kindness would be far more effectual in restraining them, and rendering them obedient, than the use of such deadly weapons. Every planter on the bayou should frown upon such inhumanity."[8]

What Solomon experiences as a heroic defense of his humanity is little more than Ford's attempt to give Tibeats a more workable strategy for manipulating the enslaved to comply with their forced servitude. Ford clearly understands that his calculated strategy of provisionally acknowledging black humanity not only encourages his enslaved charges to be more compliant and, by turn, better workers (recall Solomon's gratitude toward Ford led to him to create a cheap alternative for transporting Ford's lumber to market, saving Ford a small fortune in transportation costs), but it also supplies him with the cultural capital of feeling like a good master.[9] Solomon confirms Ford's lovable-racist status in the most stunning fashion when he describes his enslavement under Ford as "the bright side of slavery" and further intimates that he wouldn't have minded being Ford's slave for life if he had the benefit of being near his family: "I think of [Master Ford] with affection, and had my family been with me, could have borne his gentle servitude, without murmuring, all my days."[10]

Though Solomon makes only a few references to Mrs. Ford in the slave narrative, his depictions of her as a lovable racist are as politically significant as those of Mr. Ford. What is particularly striking about his rendering of Mrs. Ford as a lovable racist is that it comes at the direct expense of othering and erasing Eliza's humanity as a woman and mother. Even as *Twelve Years* decries Eliza's cruel treatment during the slave auction under the thumb of Freeman, it substantially shifts focus when Eliza falls under the care of the Ford family. In keeping with the lovable-racist mindset of the text, Solomon tell us in chapter 7 that Ford "tried to console" Eliza when she arrived on his plantation by telling her "that she need not work very hard"[11] and making her a house slave—a coveted status within slavery because it meant that one would eat better and avoid the harsh toll of laboring under the elements and an overseer's lash. (Of course, as Harriet Jacobs reminds us in *Incidents in the Life of a Slave Girl* being a house slave also made the enslaved—especially women—more vulnerable to violence and sexual assault.) Suffice it to say, when Eliza moves to the Ford plantation, we are prompted as readers to see her being properly attended to and cared for. Eliza's subsequent and unrelenting mourning for her children—mourning which draws the ire of Mrs. Ford—is thus recast within Solomon's lovable-racist mindset as unwarranted, if not a sign of ungratefulness. When next we hear of Eliza in chapter 8 she has been sold and Solomon runs into her at another plantation in the bayou. He opines, Eliza "had not pleased Mrs. Ford, being more occupied in brooding over her sorrows than in attending to her business, and had, in consequence, been sent down to work in the field on the plantation."[12] Without regard for the legitimacy of Eliza's mourning and humanity or, equally as crucial, Mrs. Ford's callousness and inhumanity, Solomon notes Eliza "had grown feeble and emaciated, and was still mourning her children." He concludes, "She had sunk beneath the weight of an excessive grief. Her drooping form and hollow cheeks too plainly indicated that she had well nigh reached the end of her weary road."[13] Slavery emerges here as a disembodied disease that has crushed Eliza's soul. The cause of Eliza's suffering (namely, the Fords' indifference to her trauma as a mother and intolerance of her depressive state) is never at issue.

When next we encounter Mrs. Ford—following Solomon's near-death experience after fighting with Tibeats—Solomon is praising her for being so gentle and motherly toward him. The disconnect between his portrait of Eliza's denied motherhood (which he attributes, in large part, to Eliza's ungratefulness to the Fords) and Mrs. Ford's state-sanctioned white supremacist motherhood is rather unsettling. Wanting to repay the Fords for protecting him from being lynched (and presumably Mrs. Ford, in particular, for "allowing" him to sleep on the floor in her house as an extra precaution against Tibeats returning to the plantation after dark to finish the job), Solomon, who is barely able to move from the severe beating he takes while being strung up, begins to weed the Fords' garden the following morning. He experiences Mrs. Ford's insistence that he rest and that weeding her garden was beyond the scope of his obligations as an exceptional display of kindness. He refers to her admiringly as "gentle", "generous," and "my protectress." Acting in many ways as a surrogate of white male patriarchy, Solomon reifies the southern myth of the southern belle. That is, he prompts the reader to see Mrs. Ford as the embodiment of Victorian womanhood. She is physically beautiful, gentle, and kind, and she exudes Christian piety. Seemingly lost on Solomon is that she is a slaver as well—that his condition of suffering and, certainly that of Eliza, whom she has sold off out of malice, is directly tied to her privilege as a white woman and her willful participation in white patriarchal supremacy. What's more, Solomon does not extend the same level of consideration toward Eliza, who has suffered an unspeakable trauma, in part, because Mrs. Ford does not relate to her humanity as a woman and mother. Indeed, her status within white patriarchy as a woman and mother depends parasitically on this misidentification.

Even though Solomon's portrait of Mrs. Epps is decidedly more complicated—he registers her cruelty against Patsey—he maintains adherence to lovable-racist thinking. Rather than hold her accountable for her calculated brutality and gross abuses of power, he characterizes her as a southern belle and blames Master Epps and the institution of slavery for corrupting her "natural" character. To wit, after detailing Mrs. Epps's hatred of Patsey ("To be rid of Patsey . . . by sale, or death, or in any manner . . . seemed to be the ruling thought and passion of my Mistress") Solomon then qualifies his critique by presenting the institution of slavery and her heartless tyrant of a husband as the culprits of her hate. He informs the reader that Mrs. Epps "was not naturally such an evil woman, after all. She was possessed of the devil, jealousy, it is true, but aside from that, there was much in her character to admire." He then expounds on her pedigree. We learn that her father was an influential and "honorable" man and that she was well educated, "beautiful, accomplished and usually good-humored." He avers, "In a different society from that which exists on the shores of Bayou Boeuf, she would have been pronounced an elegant and fascinating woman. An ill wind it was that blew her into the arms of Epps."[14] So even as Solomon is highly critical of Mrs. Epps's treatment of Patsey, he is conspicuously careful to register her humanity and the complexity of her relationship with Patsey. She is a southern belle who, absent her husband's wicked obsession with Patsey, unspeakable cruelty, and barbaric behavior, could have easily embodied the Victorian ideal.

Even as Solomon delineates Patsey in sympathetic ways in relationship to her mistreatment under Mrs. Epps, he repeats a pattern of parasitical othering (as discussed earlier between Mrs. Ford and Eliza) which obscures rather than enhances our understanding of black women's complex humanity. He describes Patsey as a "simple-minded slave . . . in whose heart God had implanted seeds of virtue." He further notes that she "was a splendid animal, and were it not that bondage had enshrouded her intellect in utter and everlasting darkness, would have been chief among ten thousand of her people."[15] Extending the animal metaphor, he notes, "She could leap the highest fences, and a fleet hound it was indeed, that could outstrip her in a race. No horse could fling her from their back. . . . Such lighting-like motion was in her fingers as no other fingers ever possessed, and therefore it was, that in cotton picking time, Patsey was queen of the field."[16]

While it is clear that Solomon is trying to be complimentary, his description of Patsey emphasizes her extraordinary physical attributes to the exclusion of her humanity. Indeed, his boasting of her "redeeming" attributes, especially in the context of comparing her favorably to animals like dogs, mules, and horses, conjures up an auction block. Such hyper-primitive and hyper-animalistic attributes also recall the extant idea of Africa as otherworldly, dangerous, untamed, undeveloped, and perpetually uncivilized. Patsey's supposed royalty is (dis)qualified within the context of Africa as a space outside of history, civilization, and industrialization. Moreover, by comparing her favorably to labor-producing animals rather than, say, to whites, women, or humans in general, he inevitably sends the message that Patsey's "value" as a human being is bound up with her value as a laborer. Even though Solomon's impulse is clearly to praise Patsey and generate empathy for her suffering under Mr. and Mrs. Epps, his rendering of her redeeming attributes succeeds more in privileging and romanticizing Mrs. Epps's white womanhood than it does in humanizing Patsey and exploding white supremacy. He is clearly using a different rubric of evaluation to discuss black women's suffering under slavery—a rubric that reinforces rather than challenges parasitical and othering models of Victorian white womanhood.

12 Years a Slave as a Corrective Intervention

Solomon's animalistic description of Patsey vis-à-vis Mrs. Epps is so star-tling that we are again stirred to question the extent and significance of David Wilson's racial fingerprint on the text. Does this strikingly dispa-rate and disturbing rendering of black/white womanhood reflect Solo-mon's unfiltered views or is it an instance of white authorial embellish-ment/alteration? If the former then what we witness here is internalized white supremacist pathology and battered slave syndrome. Solomon is not only identifying with his white oppressors to the degree to which he is evaluating black women's humanity; he is also identifying with them to the point of perpetuating the lie of benevolent slave masters and re-demptive white paternalism. If the latter is true then what we witness here is an indirect defense, if not celebration, of white moral supremacy under the guise of redemptive Victorian white womanhood. Most likely the slave narrative reflects both Solomon's lovable-racist thinking/inter-nalized white supremacist pathology and David Wilson's white autho-rial embellishment/alterations.

What the film does brilliantly is to alter our critical gaze so that we are better positioned to critically engage the limitations and problems of Solomon's lovable-racist thinking, including his blind spots regard-ing Mrs. Ford and Mrs. Epps's culpability as slavers. By putting Solomon's actions and coping strategies (including his double consciousness surviv-alist mindset) under the microscope as he does, Ridley highlights Solo-mon's complex humanity in his flaws, missteps, political naiveté, and misguided faith in white paternalism and good slave masters. As such we are usefully encouraged to see white supremacist slavery as the patho-logically driven institution that it was and to put Solomon's response to this institution in better context.

While the award-winning film *12 Years a Slave* has received legiti-mate criticism from African American scholar-activists like bell hooks and Carol Boyce Davies, who for varying reasons see his depictions of black women as overly deterministic and disempowering,[17] iconic black feminist/womanist Alice Walker, black feminist public intellectual Me-lissa Harris-Perry, and powerhouse celebrity feminist Oprah Winfrey have uniformly praised it.[18] Anecdotally speaking, the groundswell of support from black women for actress Lupita Nyong'o (who won an Oscar for Best Actress in a Supporting Role for playing Patsey and who has been outspoken about black women and the lingering effects of rac-ism/colorism) suggests that Walker, Perry, and Winfrey's perspectives are representative of how most blacks and black women specifically receive the film. The black receptivity of the film notwithstanding, my argument of the film as a useful corrective intervention vis-à-vis the slave narrative is premised upon Ridley's ostensible aim to remain true to the narrative trajectory of the text—a goal which explains why the women in the film are cast in largely supportive roles. While Ridley does not deviate from the slave narrative *Twelve Years* by introducing new black women characters or reimagining supportive characters as central ones, he develops the black women characters, and Eliza in particular, in such complex ways that they become the most insightful interrogators of white male supremacist ideology embodied in lovable-racist figures like the Fords. Moreover, the supportive cast of black women also exposes the extent to which Solomon has internalized this ideology to the point of blindness and suffers from "battered slave syndrome." Indeed, the most revealing moments in the film, as it concerns white male supremacist ideology, white paternalism, and lovable racists, directly or indirectly involve the black women characters.

While the film abounds with interrogations of white supremacist pathology, lovable-racist thinking, and battered slave syndrome via black women characters, this chapter will highlight those that most usefully trouble Solomon's critical gaze in the slave narrative, especially as it involves the lovable-racist portraits of the Fords and his warped view of white paternalism in general. Moreover, this chapter underscores the ways in which Ridley's intervention rightly encourages us to see Solomon's blind faith in paternalistic white slave owners, like the Fords, in the slave narrative as a symptom of living in a pathologically white supremacist and terrorist-driven society. Ridley's choice to recast Eliza as a self-actualized and politically shrewd subject within the lovable-racist logic of white paternalism bears out this unique phenomenon. Ridley not only equips Eliza with a voice to express her feelings of anguish, pain, resentment, and anger as a mother whose children have been forcefully taken from her and sold, but he does so in such a way as to encourage the viewers to question rather than embrace Solomon's lovable-racist thinking, especially as it concerns the Fords' culpability as slavers. Ridley clears the way for Eliza's intervention by having Mrs. Ford, the embodiment of Victorian womanhood in the slave narrative, expose the parasitical terms of her white woman privilege when she first encounters Eliza, who, fresh from the slave market, is crying inconsolably about the traumatizing theft of her children. Upon learning the source of Eliza's grief from Mr. Ford, Mrs. Ford intones empathetically to Mr. Ford, "Poor, poor woman," and then tells Eliza, "Something to eat and some rest; your children will soon enough be forgotten."[19] Mrs. Ford's complicity as a slaver in dehumanizing Eliza is unmistakable. Belying the portrait of Victorian white womanhood that Solomon offers in the slave narrative, Mrs. Ford is cold and calculating. Her words of comfort to Eliza—no doubt experienced by Mrs. Ford as genuine and heartfelt—come across to the critical viewer as what they actually are: words designed to pacify and manipulate Eliza into accepting her subordinate social and human status. Indeed, Mrs. Ford's perky delivery and optimistic tone draw the viewer's attention to the underlying cruelty and pathology of white supremacist logic during slavery. Mrs. Ford treats Eliza's trauma of being forcefully separated from her children—an act of cruelty that the Fords have a direct hand in facilitating—as little more than a headache that can be remedied with a warm meal and a good night of rest.

What's crucial to note in this scene, beyond how it exposes the parasitical relationship of Victorian white womanhood to enslaved black womanhood, is that the cruelty of Mrs. Ford's words and her complicity in slavery are not lost on Eliza. Rather than accommodate the Fords' expectation for her to internalize her suffering and treat their faux gestures of empathy as authentic, Eliza openly and unapologetically mourns the theft of her children. As discussed earlier, the slave narrative treats Eliza's mourning as a sign of ungratefulness, but the film flips the script, so to speak, and redirects our attention to the complicity of the Fords in slavery and dehumanization and to the redemptive defiance of Eliza's refusal to tamp down or hide her mourning for her stolen children. What Eliza's redemptive defiance also exposes is the degree to which Solomon's investment in white paternalism and lovable racists like Mr. Ford is bankrupt and self-defeating.

To heighten the significance of Eliza's critical perspective, Ridley strategically juxtaposes scenes in which the Fords are unnerved by Eliza's unapologetic and loud weeping with scenes in which Solomon attempts to impress Ford and defy Tibeats via his laboring assignment chopping timber near the swamp. Prior to Solomon's invention of a raft to transport Ford's lumber across the swamp, Ridley intersperses a scene in which Ford is reading from the Bible as the camera spans from Mr. Ford to Mrs. Ford and then from Eliza to Solomon. Mrs. Ford's facial expressions and body language communicate her disgust with Eliza's mourning and anticipate her eventual decision to sell her off. Lest we miss the significance of Mrs. Ford's parasitical relationship to Eliza and black womanhood, Ridley has Ford read biblical passages from Matthew, chapter 19, which highlight the disconnect between his inhuman actions as a slaver and his religious teachings. The passage conveys that the "greatest

commandments" of the Judeo-Christian faith is for Christians to extend
to each other (and presumably non-Christians) the gracious love that
the "morally perfect" Christian god bestows to his morally imperfect
human charges. Indeed, the passage is about affirming and defending
humanity and the godly wrath that will result from not doing so. The reality is that the teachings are for the enslaved, which is to say the teachings are designed explicitly to reinforce white supremacy and black/
African inferiority. Slave masters are situated within the white supremacist paternalist calculus as parental messiahs who are in many ways not
beholden to the religious doctrine that they preach. (Indeed, the Bible's
doublespeak on slavery—wherein slaves are advised to obey their masters even as such superior/subordinate statuses are supposedly meaning-
less in the eyes of the Almighty—lends itself nicely to this imperialist
conditioning.) The conspicuous clash in the scene between Mr. Ford's
biblical reading of human compassion, love, and empathy, Eliza's au-
dible crying for the loss of her children, and Mrs. Ford's visible discomfort throws light on the practice of using Christianity to promote white
supremacy/black inferiority and, by extension, to justify slavery. Here,
Ridley exposes how a white supremacist version of Christianity undermines the expressed level of empathy in equality that the biblical passages promote. What becomes clear is that religion is the discourse by
and through which traumas of the kind that Eliza is suffering are erased
or explained away.

Ridley directly engages this phenomenon of white supremacist religious conditioning and erasure in the argument that erupts between
Eliza and Solomon in the next scene. Prior to the argument, Mr. Ford
rewards Solomon with a violin for his innovative and tremendous cost-
saving lumber transportation idea. The affirmation Solomon receives
from being acknowledged and praised by Mr. Ford is unmistakable. He
gladly and humbly accepts the gift. The problem with Eliza arises when
Solomon's empathy with the Fords compels him to try to silence Eliza
in the name of looking out for her best interest. At dinner that evening
Solomon becomes annoyed with Eliza's crying to the point of violence.
After imploring her to stop crying several times to no avail, he yells
forcefully: "Stop it! Stop it!" Eliza retorts defiantly, crying is "all I have to
keep my loss present." Solomon warns that her sorrow will become her
undoing. Acutely aware of his warped racial consciousness and desire
to accommodate the Fords, Eliza turns the tables and asks why he *isn't*
crying for his children. Shifting the focus to the Fords' dehumanizing
position and the problems of accommodating their twisted notions of
themselves as loving and caring slavers, Eliza's statement shines light on

Solomon's complicity in oppression, the reality of which he clearly is unprepared to come to grips with. When he acknowledges that his loss is as painful as hers, she exposes his silencing attempt as a form of white supremacist policing: "Then who is distressed? Do I upset the Mistress and the Master? Do you care less for my loss than their well being?" Exposing his double consciousness survivalist mindset, Solomon responds, "Master Ford is a decent man." The argument then escalates:

ELIZA: "He is a slaver."

SOLOMON: "Under the circumstances . . ."

ELIZA: "Under the circumstances he is a slaver! Christian only in his proclamations. But you truckle at his boot—"

SOLOMON: "No . . ."

ELIZA: "You luxuriate in his favor."

SOLOMON: "I survive. I will not fall into despair. Woeful and crushed; melancholy is the yolk I see most. I will offer up my talents to Master Ford. I will keep myself hearty until freedom is opportune."

ELIZA: "Ford is your opportunity? Do you think he does not know that you are more than you suggest? But he does nothing for you. Nothing. You are no better than prized livestock. Call for him. Call, tell him of your previous circumstances and see what it earns you . . . *Solomon*."

Even though Solomon imagines himself to be subversive—currying favor with Mr. Ford in hopes that he can later appeal for his freedom—Eliza exposes his warped admiration for Ford and anticipates the inevitable outcome of disappointment and further exploitation. We witness this dynamic in the above passage when she refers to him flippantly by his real name, Solomon, versus his slave name, Platt. Her argument is difficult to refute. If Solomon thinks so highly of the Fords then why doesn't he tell them the truth about his kidnapping? If, indeed, Ford is the "decent" man of integrity that Solomon depicts him to be, then Ford would most certainly set him free upon learning of his circumstances.

Eliza is not condemning Solomon for his desire to stay in the Fords' good graces so much as warning him not to confuse their provisional acknowledgment of his humanity as a genuine display of kindness and humanity. The Fords see Solomon first and foremost as a slave and their treatment toward him, however humane it might appear, is ultimately self-serving and contingent upon his productivity and obedience as a laborer. Eliza's insights on the Fords and Solomon's lovable-racist mindset come from experience. As she confesses to Solomon as her anger wanes: "I too have done so many, many dishonorable things to survive. And for all of them I have ended up here. No better than if I had stood up for myself. Father, Lord and Savior forgive me. . . . Forgive me. Oh, Solomon, let me weep for my children." Beyond exposing how he romanticizes the Fords as lovable racists and "good masters," Eliza's argument with Solomon highlights the extent to which she is acutely aware that her grieving disturbs the Fords; that it serves as a constant reminder that they are chiefly responsible for the loss of her children and freedom. This sharp ideological point of departure from the slave narrative, in which the Fords are elevated to hero status and Eliza reduced to an ungrateful slave, encourages the viewer to see Ford's culpability and Solomon's racial blind spots and unconscious complicity in oppression.

To underscore the significance of this crucial moment in the film, Ridley bookends the argument with another sermon scene that usefully discredits the lovable-racist portrait of the Fords presented in the text version. In the scene Mr. Ford reads a biblical passage from Luke, chapter 18, about the Christian god's protective stance regarding children: "But who so shall offend one of these little ones which believe in me, it were better for him that a millstone were hanged about his neck, and that he were drowned in the depth of the sea." The cruel irony of the biblical passage is not lost on the viewer. The Fords experience their dehumanization and exploitation of the enslaved, which includes traumatizing Eliza and her children, as benevolent paternalism. As discussed earlier, antebellum versions of Christianity in the South were designed ostensibly to propagate white supremacy/paternalism, relieve white slavers of their guilt and culpability, and encourage the enslaved to accept their subordinate status. Ridley draws the viewers' attention to this reprehensible pattern of manipulation by having the sound of Eliza's crying disrupt and overpower the flow and political sentiment of the sermon. Mrs. Ford conveys the threat Eliza's unapologetic mourning poses to the intensely policed romance of white supremacist paternalism when she turns to an enslaved woman sitting by her side during the sermon and whispers, "I cannot have that kind of depression about." Whereas Eliza's depression in the slave narrative is understood contradictorily as both a consequence of her forced separation at the hands of Freeman and her inability to take advantage of the Fords' benevolent paternalism, the movie re-presents it as act of rebellion. By refusing to internalize her emotions, Eliza not only challenges the romance of white supremacist paternalism but she directly indicts the Fords as heartless victimizers. The scene makes clear that it is not Eliza's depression to which the Fords most object, but rather the challenges her unapologetic mourning poses to the slavocracy and white supremacist status quo. Further, Mrs. Ford's cold and calculated statement about Eliza during the sermon reveals her to be an active and willful accomplice in supporting white patriarchal power and silencing black resistance. Mrs. Ford's comments during the sermon leave no doubt that she plays an active role in having Eliza sold off.

Ridley also registers the significance of Eliza's intervention when Solomon tries to reveal his true identity to Mr. Ford, following his near lynching at the hands of Tibeats. When Solomon tells Mr. Ford, "you must know . . . I am not a slave," Mr. Ford shuts him down, "I cannot hear that." Indeed, his chief concern is protecting his economic interest, which is why he talks exclusively of *his* sacrifices and scolds Solomon for putting him in such a tough predicament: "I am trying to save your life! And . . . I have a debt to be mindful of. That, now, is to Edwin Epps. He is a hard man. Prides himself on being a 'nigger breaker.' But truthfully I could find no others who would have you. You've made a reputation of yourself. Whatever your circumstances, you are an exceptional nigger, Platt. I fear no good will come of it." We see the perversity of white paternalist slavery in Ford's conscious refusal to hear the truth about Solomon's origins. The truth of the matter—as Solomon spells out plainly—is that Ford "must know" from his high level of education and engineering expertise that Solomon was not born into slavery, wherein educating slaves was illegal. Ford's and white slavers' willful blindness is, as Eliza insinuates in her argument with Solomon, inextricably bound up in the white supremacist slave ideology.

Ridley's intervention here is important also because elevating the Fords to hero status, as the slave narrative does, necessarily requires explaining away or outright erasing Eliza's subjectivity as a woman, mother, and traumatized victim of white male supremacist slavery. What his intervention allows us to see is Eliza's agency as an interrogator of white supremacist slavery. In the slave narrative Solomon never considers the Fords' culpability. Or rather he explains away their culpability as a consequence of their ideological and social conditioning. Beyond highlighting how the Fords are as culpable as any other slaver in dehumanizing and exploiting blacks, the film conveys the extent to which the Fords— via their employment of a white supremacist version of Christianity— operate consciously as policing agents of the status quo. When faced with any challenges to their white supremacist slave ideology in the form of "disobedient" or "ungrateful" slaves, the Fords respond with varying silencing strategies, as is clearly the case with Eliza. Even though Mr. Ford desires to keep Solomon, aka Platt, he is not willing to take the financial risk of harboring an outspoken, self-actualized slave. As Ford informs Solomon (in the book and the film), his reputation as a "disobedient"

slave has spread across the county, meaning that he faces potential lethal action from all white planters, not just from Tibeats. As Ford's white
supremacist selfhood depends parasitically on not seeing or acknowledging the humanity of Solomon and other blacks, he has no interest in
knowing what he intuitively already knows about the truth of Solomon's
claims. The truth, as it were, is bad for business and, as Mr. Ford relays to
Solomon, "I have a debt to be mindful of."

In terms of Ridley's exposing Ford's lovable-racist status in the slave
narrative and, more specifically, his culpability as a slave owner, it is important to highlight how the film re-scripts the auction scene with Eliza.
As previously established, Solomon presents Ford as a kind and mer-
ciful man in the slave narrative, emphasizing his capacity to empathize
with Eliza's suffering—empathy which, consequently, is also the basis
for Solomon's rendering of Eliza as an ungrateful slave under Ford's servitude. In the slave narrative Ford emerges as magnanimous because
his decision to purchase Eliza's daughter is driven by compassion and
empathy rather than capitalism. The reader is prompted to believe two
contradictory ideas about Ford; the first being that he is a shrewd businessman and the second being that he is oblivious to the market value
of a biracial girl slave. Freeman's response of indignation to Ford's offer
and subsequent appeal to morality and family values encourages the
reader to see Freeman as the real monster and Ford as the misguided,
lovable slave master that Solomon so admires.

The film reimagines this scene so that Ford's appeal is read within the
context of price bartering over slaves. That is, we are prompted to see
Ford as a shrewd businessman with many years of experience buying
and selling slaves, meaning that he is well aware of not only the price of
Eliza's biracial daughter but why said price is so high. Thus when he appeals to Freeman on the basis of morality and family values as a way to
get a lower price, we can better understand and appreciate why Freeman
reacts with incredulity. To indulge Ford's initial bartering ploy to buy the
girl on the basis that "one so young will bring you no profit," Freeman
explains that there are "heaps 'n piles of money to be made off her. She
is a beauty. One of the regular bloods. None of your thick-lipped, bullet
headed, cotton picking niggers." When Ford then shifts tactics and tries
to shame Freeman ("Her child, man. For God's sake, are you not senti-
mental in the least?"), Freeman responds with justifiable indignation.
That is, he is rightly offended by Ford's appeal to morality and family
values as a slaver. Freeman not only calls Ford on his insulting bartering
ploy ("My sentimentality stretches the length of a coin"); he also gives
him an ultimatum and shuts down debate ("Do you want the lot . . . or

do you pass on them all?"). Ford's abrupt shift in tone from moral outrage to compliance ("I will take the ones Platt and Eliza") reflects the insincerity of his appeals to morality and family values. Ridley clearly conveys that Ford is a calculating businessman. While the transaction is not ideal for Ford in terms of what it potentially means for Eliza's morale and productivity as a worker, his ultimate decision to buy her demonstrates that separating mother from child is not a deal breaker. By having Freeman call Ford's bluff and expose Ford's decision to buy Eliza as ultimately self-interested, Ridley obliterates the idea in the slave narrative that Ford possesses a higher moral compass than other slavers.

Out of the Shadows of Black Men's Pain

We established early in the chapter that Solomon's attempt in the slave narrative to generate empathy for Patsey is limited in large part because he creates a separate rubric of evaluation of black women's humanity vis-à-vis white women. Patsey is described as "simple-minded" and compared "favorably" to animals whereas Mrs. Epps, who is savage, cruel, and barbaric in her treatment toward Patsey, is described as beautiful, sophisticated, and generally good-spirited (except in relation to Patsey) and compared favorably to other high society white women and the Victorian womanhood ideal. While the Victorian ideal is certainly problematic on many levels, not the least of which being that the standard of ideal womanhood in the antebellum era was premised on white patriarchal notions of chastity and commodification, it allows for white women to have provisional power and status within the white patriarchal power structure. Moreover, white women derive their social agency as women who are worthy of white patriarchal protection and honor in direct opposition to black women, whose patriarchal womanhood, in terms of being chaste and worthy of patriarchal protection, is always already obliterated. Black women cannot be chaste, according to white patriarchal thinking, because they are savage, animalistic, and without moral boundaries. This is the thinking that white slavers employed to explain away white male rape. Though white men possessed the legal, political, and material means to force black women to comply with their sexual desires, they cultivated a mindset of black women as savage, sexual beings and white men as innocent paternalist victims to displace the blame of rape onto black women—a move that bespoke a deeper emotional, if not psychological, need to justify human atrocities within their white circles.[20] White women, by turn, were complicit in this white male supremacist victim blaming to the degree to which they (mis)directed their anger, fears, and anxieties about their husbands' sexual exploitation of enslaved black women onto black women.

Zora Neale Hurston famously illustrates this phenomenon of displacement and white women's brutality against black women in *Their Eyes Were Watching God* by the reaction that the mistress of Nanny's plantation (whom Nanny calls "Madam") has to the "white" appearance of Nanny's child. When Madam becomes increasingly violent as she repeatedly asks Nanny (who has just birthed a child fathered by Madam's husband and the master of the plantation) why does her child look white, Nanny (who understands the race-gender politics behind the question and also the high stakes involved in being the focus of white women's jealousy) responds that she is "uh nigger and uh slave" who "don't know nothin' but what Ah'm told tuh do."[21] Rather than generate empathy from Madam, who is also the legal property of her husband via the antebellum laws of coverture, Nanny's earnest appeal for empathy as a vulnerable subject of white male power only provokes Madam to a murderous rage. She threatens to beat Nanny to death and sell off her child. Nanny only avoids this fate by fleeing to nearby swamps and hiding out until the Union soldiers take over the plantation.

Even as the slave narrative *Twelve Years* is attentive to the ways that white patriarchal power contributes to the tensions between enslaved black women and white women, it explains away Mrs. Epps and other white women's provisional agency and white privilege within the patriarchal slavocracy. Keep in mind, Mrs. Epps tries repeatedly to bribe/coax Solomon into murdering Patsey whenever Master Epps is away from the plantation on business. Though Solomon never spells out if he faced serious consequences from Mrs. Epps for refusing her requests, we can safely assume there probably weren't any given that her actions were working directly against the economic well-being of her household and, more generally, the economic calculus of white patriarchal slavocracy. In addition to letting Mrs. Epps off the hook for her provisional agency, white privilege, and culpability in oppression, the slave narrative's disparate portraits of Mrs. Epps and Patsey substantiates, albeit indirectly, the idea of Patsey and other black women as tough, savage, strong and hypersexual and white women as delicate, sensitive, smart and blameless. What we end up with is a portrait of Patsey that is inherently contradictory; she is primitive, strong, athletic, and a potential tribal leader and she is also simple-minded, vulnerable, weak, and tragic. On display here is Solomon's inability to imagine Patsey or black women in general as complex human beings and race-gender subjects beyond the white male gaze and economies of slavery.

12 Years usefully intervenes in this regard, positioning Mrs. Epps as the true savage and encouraging the viewers to see Patsey's complex humanity. The film accomplishes this task without ignoring the political and economic reality of white women's commodification within the white patriarchal order. This reality is borne out when, during one of Master Epps's late night dance parties, Mrs. Epps becomes infuriated with her husband (who openly displays his lust for Patsey while she dances) and demands that he sell Patsey. When Master Epps dismisses the request out of hand—"You're talkin foolish"—Mrs. Epps threatens to leave him. Calling her bluff, Master Epps reminds her that he "rescued" her through marriage from her previous small-town life existence in Cheneyville. He then issues his own threat: "Do not set yourself up against Patsey, my dear. That's a wager on which you will not profit. Calm yerself. And settle for my affection, 'cause affection you got. Or, go. 'Cause I will rid myself of yah well before I do away with her!"[22] Tellingly, he speaks of his marriage and relationship to Patsey in decidedly economic terms. Mrs. Epps "will not profit" from trying to strong-arm him to sell Patsey because in the grand scheme of things Patsey, as a laborer and concubine, is to Master Epps a more valuable commodity than his wife. Moreover, the laws of coverture meant that men ultimately benefited from divorce because, as the property of their husbands, women who chose to divorce their husbands, or whose husbands divorced them, were not entitled to property or even the custody of their children. Not to mention that divorced women faced a host of social stigmas as their social value as women was largely defined through marriage, child rearing, and the like.

What the film's attentiveness to white women's subjugation under white patriarchal power in slavery brings sharply into focus is that despite this phenomenon of white women as the property of their husbands, the overwhelming majority of white women did not see natural allies in enslaved and sexually exploited black women. To the contrary, in fact. If anything, white women invested ample time and energy into distinguishing themselves from enslaved black women, as their value and status as white women in a white patriarchal society rested upon their not-black-womanness. Which is to say, their value and status as white women relied on their being understood and treated within the white patriarchal order as chaste, feminine, nurturing, obedient (to men), Christian, and domestically industrious.

Rather than a victim of white patriarchal power, Mrs. Epps emerges in the film as one of its staunchest defenders. She warns her husband time and again that blurring the lines between master and slave, in terms of intimacy and power, presented a clear and present danger. To dispel the notion that her warning is merely a thinly camouflaged indictment of his sexual relationship with (read: rape of) Patsey, Ridley includes a scene in which Mrs. Epps interrogates Solomon about his origins, manners, and reading behaviors. Her message is as clear as it is chilling. If he wanted to stay alive and in the good graces of his master and mistress he needed to refrain from reading or writing and continue to hide the details of his origins. In short, she was as invested in the socioeconomic spoils of slavery as her husband and equally as willing, if not more so, to employ the brutal, terrorist-style violence necessary to maintain the status quo. By suggesting via his lovable-racist narration in the slave narrative that Mrs. Epps's hatred toward Patsey is ultimately the fault of Master Epps, Solomon obscures the political, economic, and social stakes for (elite) white women operating within and benefiting from white patriarchal slavocracy. In stark contrast, the film calls our attention to the economic and social vulnerability of even an elite woman, like Mrs. Epps, but does so in such a way as to highlight her complicity in the oppression of white women and enslaved blacks. What we see in Mrs. Epps's contempt for Patsey is not simply the result of jealousy (as in she views the sexual relationship as a form of infidelity), but also the result of fear. As her capacity to exercise power over Patsey and other enslaved blacks is bound up in her relationship to Master Epps and white patriarchal power, Patsey's "privileged" status in Master Epps's eyes threatens to undermine the provisional power at her disposal as the wife of a slaver. In the film Mrs. Epps attempts to restore her power by stoking her husband's insecurities as a slaver of losing control of his slaves. Moreover, Mrs. Epps uses his twisted jealousy toward Patsey to incite him to violence against the latter. Indeed, the brutal beating Patsey receives from the (forced) hands of Solomon and then Mr. Epps for traveling without permission to the Shaw plantation for soap (which, consequently, Mrs. Epps withholds from her out of spite) stems in large part from Mrs. Epps egging her jealous husband on. Rather than encourage her to empathize with the enslaved, Mrs. Epps's subordinate gendered status within white patriarchal slave culture prompts her to defend what limited agency/privilege she possesses as a white woman. The film demonstrates that despite her subjugation under white patriarchal slave culture, Mrs. Epps is an active and willful participant in the domination of the enslaved. Paradoxically, her gendered subjugation intensifies instead of tempers her policing of the status quo.

In the final analysis, the film *12 Years* reminds us of how important it is for African Americans and oppressed groups in general to tell our stories without fear, manipulation, or political pressure. Predictably, the film's success has sparked renewed interest in the slave narrative on which it is based. While this renewed interest is ultimately a good outcome because slavery remains a woefully understudied and misunderstood aspect of our cultural history, there are crucial blind spots in the narrative, as we have seen, which distort white culpability and reinforce aspects of white supremacist pathology. As Frederick Douglass reminds us time and again throughout *The Narrative*, the term "good slave master" is an oxymoron. Anyone who enslaves another, regardless of the terms of that enslavement, is guilty of a human atrocity. Edward P. Jones makes this point brilliantly in *The Known World* when the narrator expounds on black slave-cum-slave owner Henry Townsend's aspirations to be a better master than white men: "He did not understand the kind of world he wanted to create was doomed before he had even spoken the first syllable of the word *master*."[23] Henry's imagined world of compassionate black slave owners is doomed from the outset because enslaving human beings (even if you are black and were once a slave yourself) is by definition oppressive and inhumane. The danger, then, of the slave narrative *Twelve Years* is that it not only imagines the possibility of good slave masters but stridently defends the position. Such ideas are, indeed, a matter of life and death in a country where white fears of black/brown bodies often serve to legitimize hypersurveillance in black/brown communities, such as stop-and-frisk programs, and the indiscriminate use of lethal force, such as Stand Your Ground laws. That said, the film's popularity and the fact that we now exist in a visual culture all but guarantees that significantly more people will screen the film than read the slave narrative. Though as a scholar I would strongly advocate putting text and film into critical dialogue as I have attempted to do here, I certainly won't lose any sleep over the fact that most people will only see the movie.

TWO

Constituting the Crime: White Innocence as an Apparatus of Oppression

Innocence defined nineteenth century childhood, and not vice versa; therefore, as popular culture purged innocence from representations of African American children, the black child was redefined as a non-child—a "pickaninny." The pickaninny was an imagined, subhuman black juvenile who was typically depicted outdoors, merrily accepting (or even inviting) violence. ROBIN BERNSTEIN

Something rather stunning happens at the end of Toni Morrison's gruesome description of Sethe's infanticide in *Beloved* (1987). As readers will recall, the scene is rendered largely through slave owner schoolteacher's chilling perspective. Warped as he is by white supremacist ideology and unspeakable acts of human cruelty, schoolteacher does not see the inhumanity of his behavior toward Sethe and enslaved Africans. Instead of recognizing the causality of the human tragedy of Sethe's infanticide for what it is— namely, a psychotic break brought on by the stresses and traumas of slavery—schoolteacher sees only the financial loss. His only acknowledgment of culpability is to blame his nephew for "mishandling" of Sethe to the point of making her go "wild." The punishment meted out for the "offense" bespeaks his blindness. Schoolteacher doesn't let the nephew come along for the "hunt" and assigns him extra chores. It is, indeed, this blindness as rendered in the scene that magnifies and frames the black tragedy.

Grandmother to the four children whom Sethe has tried to kill out of a lethal motherly impulse, Baby Suggs is somehow able to rein in her emotions and negotiate with Sethe to make her hand over the crawling-already baby who, throat slit to nearly the point of decapitation, has bled out in Sethe's arms and left a pool of blood in the house. Though Morrison does not provide a linear timeline, we can deduce via other events that unfold that Baby Suggs's negotiation with Sethe to retrieve the crawling-already baby is an extended affair. In the time that it finally takes Baby Suggs to get Sethe to give over the crawling-already baby she is able to bathe her two grandsons and then comfort a crying Denver in her arms. The only way that Baby Suggs gets Sethe to give up the dead child is by informing Sethe that Denver needs to nurse and offering to exchange the living child for the deceased. The scene reaches a climax when Baby Suggs becomes incensed at Sethe's refusal to wipe the crawling-already baby's blood from her breast as she nurses Denver. In the process of wrestling with her daughter-in-law to retrieve Denver, Baby Suggs slips and falls in a pool of her dead granddaughter's blood, allowing Sethe to break away and board the sheriff's cart with Denver. After gathering herself from wrestling with Sethe, who has already left the house, Baby Suggs, soiled with blood, decides to chase after the cart that is carrying Sethe and Denver to jail in hopes of trying to protect and retrieve her surviving granddaughter. As Baby Suggs attempts to run after Sethe, she is stopped dead in her tracks at her doorstep by two white children—a conspicuously clueless red-haired boy who bears a striking resemblance in personality to Mark Twain's Huckleberry Finn and a more vaguely rendered blond-haired girl who does not speak. They have orders from their mother to get Baby Suggs, a shoe cobbler by trade, to fix a pair of shoes. The boy, who is munching on a sweet pepper in the midst of all the blood and gore, barks orders at Baby Suggs: "Mama says Wednesday. . . . She says you got to have these [shoes] fixed by Wednesday."[1] When an emotionally reeling Baby Suggs fails initially to reply, the boy repeats his command with rehearsed authority: "She says Wednesday, you hear? Baby? Baby?" The narrator reports: "She took the shoes from him—high topped and muddy—saying, 'I beg your pardon. Lord, I beg your pardon. I sure do.'"[2]

This rarely discussed scene engages the dangerous myth of white innocence that has been operational culturally for centuries and continues to inform who counts as fully human in US society today. The myth of white innocence derives historically and culturally from a sustained white impulse to deny white historical atrocities against enslaved Africans, "Indians," and indigenous Chicano populations. With an eye toward understanding the current utility and tenacity of the myth of white innocence, this chapter will examine several mediums, including news media, politics, and entertainment, that invoke or appropriate the myth with high frequency and, in many instances, with lethal consequence. I argue that the extant myth of white innocence functions on many levels to obscure the systemic ways in which white privilege and power are passed down from one generation to the next. The fact that we are still debating whether the undeniable racial slur Redskins (as in the Washington Redskins professional football team) should be removed as a team name, or, for that matter, that the practice of red face (think the white Florida State University mascot) is not only harmless but *honors*[3] the Seminole Indian heritage, is a striking case in point. And, to be clear, the only reasons that sport teams in the current era refrain from using racial slurs referring to African American, Jewish, Latin/ Chicano Americans, or Asians as team names/mascots is due almost entirely to the fact that these groups have the power, population, and resources (unlike most existing Native American tribes, who have never fully recovered from historical genocidal western assault, forced relocation, and economic disfranchisement) to prevent this from happening. Or, to state the matter more accurately, these groups have the power, population, and resources to prevent this long-standing practice of employing racist team names from happening *again*. The key point here is that myths of white innocence are in the aggregate steeped in a history of white violence and denial. The reality is that for most of the time that Africans (as captives) were in the United States, white children (especially the elite) were rightly perceived, if not alternately envied, despised, revered, and resented by blacks, as dominators or oppressors-in-training. Through this same historical trajectory, black children, who by all accounts constituted the weakest and most vulnerable population in the United States, were perceived and treated by whites as thugs, maids, concubines, or, more recently, (male) sport studs in training.

In the *Beloved* scene above we see how this parasitical dynamic of white innocence operates to alter and, at times, dictate black agency and behavior. Morrison's decision to place these white children in Baby Suggs's path to Denver throws this parasitical, if not lethal, characteristic of white innocence radically into focus. Morrison registers the pernicious consequences of this parasitical relationship via the carefree and oblivious nature of the children, especially the boy. Though Morrison doesn't provide the reader with the ages of the children, one would guess from the boy's verbal interaction with Baby Suggs that he is at least ten years old. Which is to say, that he is old enough and mature enough to recognize that something is terribly amiss at Baby Suggs's house. Indeed, it is almost inconceivable that the children could walk through an emotionally intense crowd of black onlookers and then witness Baby Suggs in a state of emotional panic—and presumably covered in blood—and not have at least asked her or someone in the crowd to explain the commotion. By juxtaposing the panicked, traumatized, and blood-soaked Baby Suggs against the carefree and domineering white children, Morrison calls attention on one level to the everydayness of black suffering. The white children's inexplicable blindness to the bloodshed and suffering around them is itself an indication of the perverse normalcy of white oppression and black dehumanization. That said, this scene also exposes and interrogates the long-standing political currency of white innocence, especially as it informs and complicates black consciousness and emotional agency. What becomes clear is that the children's carefreeness and blindness come at the direct expense of Baby Suggs's self-determination, emotional stability, and self-respect. The looming threat of white power embodied in the children is unmistakable. Though the very life of her beloved grandchild is at stake, Baby Suggs instinctually stops in her tracks when she opens the door to the white children. Even such high stakes are not enough to propel Baby Suggs beyond the threat of white power that the children embody. What she knows intuitively, if not also from direct experience, is that any perceived act of aggression, such as yelling at them to move or shooing them physically out of her way, is likely to spark white violence or even death. Baby Suggs, then, has little choice but to stop and attend to their trivial requests for a shoe repair. Lest we miss the significance of this scene, Morrison draws our attention to the fact that the shoes that need repairing are muddy; the whites do not even bother to clean the shoes before presenting them to Baby Suggs to fix.

Though human indignities of this kind were a daily occurrence during slavery, Morrison "mystifies the familiar"[4] for her readers by having the white children—the embodiment of white innocence—interrupt Baby Suggs's desperate attempt to rescue her granddaughter in a strikingly adult and callous way. Morrison's narrative maneuver exposes the extent to which the myth of white innocence "purifies" these white children from the domains of dehumanizing power that provides their whiteness with social and economic capital. Indeed, by delineating the incongruence between innocence and white childhood in such dramatic fashion here, Morrison shines light on white innocence as a socially constructed myth of dominant white power. Innocence is not organic to white children but rather an ideological construction of dominant white power

designed to make the relationship between white childhood and innocence appear organic. As a direct result of this socially constructed myth
of white innocence, white children (especially among the middle and
upper classes) emerge as emotionally pure, ethically blameless and even
angelic. To this end, the myth of white innocence functions like most
discourses of dominant white power—namely, its sociopolitical viability
depends on the absence-presence of othered black/brown childhood.
That said, it is the white children's display of conditioned obliviousness
to black suffering and feelings of white entitlement to black servitude
that helps the reader appreciate the limitations of Baby Suggs' and black
women's self-determination and emotional agency; emotional agency
meaning, in this instance, the ability to openly express one's emotions
without fear of white backlash. The children's actions also shine light on
the depth of white supremacist pathology and, by extension, the ethical
bankruptcy of appeals to white innocence.

As I have argued elsewhere,[5] Toni Morrison's *Beloved* seeks on a conscious level to disrupt the extant white supremacist discourse which
links pathological behavior and primitivism to Africanness and blackness. What warrants repeating for the sake of this argument is that with
this disruption—which is certainly at play in the aforementioned rendering of white innocence—Morrison's goal is not simply to contest
white supremacist hegemony which recasts whites as innocent, if not
messiah figures, and slavery as inherently beneficial to civilizing primitive Africans, but rather to contextualize present-day white supremacist
hegemony by challenging us to think differently about how power is
lived and experienced by oppressed and oppressor. In other words, Morrison employs this narrative about slavery to explain why certain domains of white power, and white patriarchal power in particular, continue
to reign supreme in the present. No doubt Morrison inserts the children
in this scene at this precise moment to expose the emotional and mental
toll that white innocence takes on black consciousness, especially for
black women. It is also hardly a coincidence that Baby Suggs personifies
what bell hooks, Michelle Wallace, Patricia Hill-Collins, and others call
strong black womanhood. The modern reader steeped in this racial romance expects Baby Suggs to soldier past such microaggressions, but in
the final analysis Morrison lets us see (and here I'm referring to Baby
Suggs's ultimate mental breakdown and subsequent death) that she is as
vulnerable as any other (white) human to violent attacks on her personhood and social stability.

As for the myth of white innocence, Morrison conveys via her rendering of the oblivious, adult-minded children that white supremacy oper-

ates ideologically to trivialize, if not erase, white culpability in dehumanizing Africans. Even though these children are not the direct cause of Baby Suggs's suffering—they have nothing logistically to do with how schoolteacher found Sethe, for example—their personhood as raced beings is tethered to white supremacist ideology and by default the perceived lack thereof of enslaved and "free" Africans. This parasitical relationship, whereby white innocence depends on black silencing, not only prevents us from seeing black humanity as such but also, more specifically, the plight of black children.

The Myth of White Innocence as a Policing Apparatus

On December 14, 2012, the unthinkable happened; a white man armed with a cache of weapons and ammunition entered an elementary school in Newtown, Connecticut, and started killing at will. When the dastardly deed was done, Adam Lanza, the shooter, had killed twenty-seven people, including twenty children and his mother (a former kindergarten teacher and volunteer at the school), whom he killed in her bed prior to arriving at the school. Adding further chaos to the situation, Lanza took his own life before the police had a chance to arrest him, leaving the families of his victims and the public at large in perpetual limbo as to why he, or anyone for that matter, would viciously murder children. Predictably, the public outcry was intense. The massacre was the second deadliest mass shooting by a single person in US history and the second deadliest mass murder at an American elementary school.[6]

Tragic though this massacre was, the unspoken, if also culturally unspeakable, reality is that our collective cultural impulse to empathize with suffering of this magnitude is color-coded. Indeed, contrary to increasingly popular notions of a postracialist America and the hoopla over the historical phenomenon of having a black president, the unspoken operating cultural mindset when it comes to who counts as worthy of empathy in our country is simply this: the experiences of (middle-class) whites is necessarily inclusive and representative of all Americans. Whiteness in the American context is the default setting, so to speak, of American citizenry. What this means in terms of lived experience of race is that whites' problems are American problems and people of color's problems are people of color's problems. (Notice how working-class identity was raced white in the public domain and their concerns—many of which were steeped in racism, xenophobia, and sexism—prioritized politically after working-class whites helped usher Donald Trump into the White House.) Racial empathy plays out in a similar way. The striking disparities in levels of racial empathy for two other crisis events—the September 11 terrorist attacks and Hurricane Katrina—bears this out. In "Do You Know What It Means . . . ? Mapping Emotion in the Aftermath of Katrina," Melissa Harris-Perry observes that while black Americans' level of mourning for the 9/11 victims was commensurate with their white peers, white Americans were strikingly unmoved by the national tragedy of Katrina compared to black Americans, who were up in arms.[7] Who can forget Kanye West's famous unscripted comments during a live televised fundraiser on NBC in 2005 for victims of Hurricane Katrina: "George Bush doesn't care about black people."[8] I suspect that most politically conscious black Americans were thinking that it was *not* just George Bush that didn't care about black people, but white America in general. Melissa Harris-Perry elucidates the racial disparity in emotional responses to both tragedies:

To be a citizen in a democracy is *to be not only the ruled, but also the ruler*. To be a citizen in a democratic republic is to have a voice in which you can name your experiences and pursue your good through public means. On September 11, the nation momentarily felt like vulnerable, attacked, but united citizens. This sense of vulnerability was less shared in the case of Katrina. Not only were the victims of the hurricane abandoned in their drowning city, but black Americans were abandoned in their grief as they once again confronted the fact of their second-class citizenship.[9]

We can deduce from Harris-Perry's sharp insights here that to be a ruled citizen in a democracy also means that you are expected to empathize with the emotional strife of the rulers but must accept that the rulers will not return this empathy in kind because your pain is somehow not as real and your concerns not as legitimate as theirs. What makes this hard to pin down ideologically is that the emotional strife of the rulers (i.e., whites and, particularly, the white middle class) is rendered in the public discourse as necessarily inclusive and, thus, universal. The racial component of white emotional strife becomes invisible within the public discourse of suffering as was the case with September 11 and Hurricane Katrina. To reiterate an earlier point, white emotional strife/suffering becomes synonymous with American suffering and strife. Which explains, to a large degree, why it is so difficult to discuss racial inflections of grief during such moments of tragedy; why those who do "go there," including whites like David Sirota (whom we will discuss momentarily), are attacked as race baiters and even anti-American rabble rousers.

Harris-Perry's critique helps us understand the interdependent relationship between white innocence and black/brown invisibility. Because the perspective of ruler-class white citizens continues to be experienced culturally as normative in such crisis moments (meaning that if you don't experience the world the same way, then you're the freak or the one who is out of touch with reality), they are rarely put in the situation of having to justify their expectation that people of color share in their pain. Likewise, whites are rarely put in the situation where they have to justify their lack of empathy for the ruled black and brown citizenry. While willful white blindness and victim blaming are certainly not new phenomena, they have been reinvigorated in the twenty-first century because certain social and economic barriers for model minorities who either reify the status quo or, at the very least, do not pose a serious threat to it have been lifted. What this means socially and politically is that a black man and model minority, like Barack Obama, can rise to the level of the presidency even as we continue to live in a two-tier system of citizenship—a system in which 1 in 5 black men are in prison compared to only 1 in 100 of white men.

What we see in the Newtown tragedy is another striking example of how this white hegemonic/ruler class empathy operates. White ruler class empathy is amplified even more so because the victims are mostly white, middle-class children. Indeed, there was a black Latino child, Ana Grace Marquez-Greene, among the children killed but she received scant coverage in the media. My guess is that most folks wouldn't remember that there were any people of color affected.

It is also critical here to point out how class intersected with race in the coverage of the Newtown tragedy to give cultural and political capital to the myth of white innocence. The dominant narrative that emerged from this tragedy pivoted on a burning question: "How could such a tragedy happen in a town like Newtown?" At first glance, this doesn't seem like an issue that has anything to do with race. Newtown is a sleepy, upper-middle-class, suburban town with a low crime rate—a kind of modern-day "Mayberry," if you will, of New England. Undergirding this question, however, is a white hegemonic narrative wherein whiteness, middle-class status, and social stability go hand in hand. The unspoken dominant culture mindset is that crimes of this magnitude *are expected* to happen in urban spaces where impoverished black and brown folks reside. This is precisely the white middle-class hegemonic narrative that emerged in 1999 after two upper-class white Columbine High School teenagers went on a killing spree at their school in Littleton,

Colorado—a town with a socioeconomic and racial makeup strikingly similar to that of Newtown. The national white crisis that erupted following both tragedies centered on how well-to-do white male students from prominent, highly educated families could commit such heinous crimes against other whites of similar backgrounds. The crisis stems in large part from the extant belief that elite whites embody the social, cultural, and economic standards (i.e., the norm) against which all other groups are measured. Because of this long-standing cultural mindset, heinous acts of white-on-white violence throw America into a social panic. This white panic stems from observing elite whites (the standard bearers of American culture) acting out in a way that is stereotypically associated with lower-class black and brown folks (the embodied cultural anti-standard bearers). We witnessed this white social panic on display in the ways in which every dominant entity from the media to Congress tried to parse out the "outside" influences that led this upper-class white boy in Newtown, Adam Lanza, to go on a shooting spree in a largely white, upper-middle-class elementary school. His status of race and class privilege is understood a priori as normal; the height of civilization. Thus, the frantic search to find the culprit of his mental and emotional unraveling starts from the operating racial premise that he started out in the world with a healthy and desirable mindset. In other words, his intersecting race and class privilege are never at issue as the *cause* of his unraveling because white superiority remains normative even though it has become largely taboo for whites to tout this cultural reality. The message this sends in the public domain regarding whiteness and children is clear; namely, that white children—even the most violent and emotionally disturbed—are deserving, not only of our love and respect, but also of our protection. Consequently, childhood innocence becomes the domain of whites only. Consider this telling fact: 107 mostly brown and black children and young adults under the age of twenty were killed in Chicago alone between March 2011 and March 2012.[10] To put this in perspective, there were almost a hundred more childhood deaths recorded during this stretch than American casualties of war in Afghanistan. So, in effect, it was safer to be an American soldier in a war zone than it was to be a black/brown child walking the streets of Southside Chicago. By all accounts, this should have been a major news story—even President Obama harped on this issue following the Newtown tragedy in a failed attempt to get Congress to pass legislation to toughen gun laws. The fact that it wasn't a major news story (The Republican Party [GOP] and the National Rifle Association [NRA] used the Chicago tragedy to argue for less regulation of guns) had everything to do with whose children were dying in the streets. It also bears mentioning that the political logjam in Congress that stalled passage of tougher gun laws following the Newtown tragedy—like requiring background checks before issuing guns or preventing folks with serious mental disorders from owning them—was not a direct reflection of how most whites felt about strengthening gun laws. As Obama touted again and again in his failed attempt to press for tougher gun laws, the overwhelming majority of American citizens, including whites in the GOP, agreed in the aftermath of the Newtown tragedy that strengthening gun laws in this way was a good idea. The cold political reality is that large corporations and lobbying entities designed to protect them are significant—and most often the *most* significant—sources of campaign fundraising for the GOP. This explains why the GOP-dominated Congress basically ignored the social sentiment and sided with the NRA and de facto lobby for the gun industry. The most pertinent point insofar as the myth of white innocence is concerned is that it took the slaughtering of white children by another white person (i.e., white-on-white crime) to alter public sentiment about gun laws and to force the powerful NRA lobby and NRA-supportive GOP to *defend* their reckless ideas about gun access and possession. In stark contrast, relatively little defense was needed on the part of the NRA and its political adherents in support of the right to bear arms when the imagined threat to white safety was a black/brown thug.

The post-Newtown gun debate aside, we witness the tenacity of the myth of white innocence in how fiercely it is protected and policed by whites. Indeed, anyone that deigns to point out the obvious—that white, middle-class bodies are valued significantly more than black and brown ones—tends to get shouted down and often labeled a racist. Observe the media firestorm that ensued, especially from the political right, when prominent white journalist David Sirota pointed out on MSNBC's "Up With Chris Hayes" show how race informed the media coverage of the event. More specifically, Sirota suggested that, if the shooter in Sandy Hook were black or a person of color, then the entire political focus point would change. Rather than addressing the possible motives for the shooting, including mental health issues and violent video games, the focus would be on the supposed criminality and violence of black men and politicians would be calling for heightened surveillance of and profiling of black men. In an op-ed, "Time to Profile White Men," Sirota elucidates his perspective on the controversy:

I said [on the "Up With Chris Hayes" Show] that because most of the mass shootings in America come at the hands of white men, there would likely be political opposition to initiatives that propose to use those facts to profile the demographic group to which these killers belong. I suggested that's the case because as opposed to people of color or, say, Muslims, white men as a subgroup are in such a privileged position in our society that they are the one group that our political system avoids demographically profiling or analytically aggregating in any real way. Indeed, unlike other demographics, white guys as a group are never thought to be an acceptable topic for any kind of critical discussion whatsoever, even when there is ample reason to open up such a discussion. My comment was in response to U.S. Rep. James Langevin (D) floating the idea of employing the Secret Service for such profiling, and I theorized that because the profiling would inherently target white guys, the political response to such an idea might be similar to the Republican response to the 2009 Homeland Security report looking, in part, at the threat of right-wing terrorism. As you might recall, the same GOP that openly supports profiling—and demonizing—Muslims essentially claimed that the DHS report was unacceptable because its focus on white male terrorist groups allegedly stereotyped (read: offensively profiled) conservatives.[11]

Sirota received so much heat from the political right (even though these issues of race cut across party lines) precisely because he is, by all counts, an elite white man. His class and race status means that his comments can't so easily be dismissed. What we know about dominant ideologies of power is that they tend to manipulate social realities so that victims of dominant power emerge as shortsighted, uninformed, whining, and irresponsible and victimizers as rational, even-tempered, just, and insightful. What this means on the ground is that the responsibility for addressing the concerns of victimized groups—be they victims of racism, sexism, homophobia, classism, or all of the above—tends to fall squarely on the shoulders of said groups. Moreover, legitimate critiques about the machinations of dominant ideologies that come from victimized groups are typically dismissed by those in power as biased. Antiracism advocates are re-presented as race baiters, angry black/brown wo/men, or "race card" pimps; feminists as man-hating lesbians or, what right-wing provocateur Rush Limbaugh calls derisively "Femi-Nazis"; and antihomophobic activists as perverts, sodomists, and social abominations, to name but a few. The rub, however, is that when the folks from the standard-bearer group (meaning straight, middle-class, educated, Christian, white men) weigh in on the side of the truly victimized, the dominant group is forced to engage with them because they wield the cultural capital of whiteness—a reality which means, more often than not, that their perspectives will be taken seriously by other whites. Which is another way of saying that their normative gender, race, class, sexuality, and religious status will greatly increase their legitimacy in the eyes of whites, despite the fact that they also constitute the very group that is chiefly responsible for creating and perpetuating these inequalities.

White Innocence, Sentimentality, and Complicity in Oppression

As we know, ideologies of power are not easily dismantled. When they face serious social, cultural, or economic challenges, as was the case with white supremacist ideology during the Civil Rights Movement, they adjust like a chameleon to the new environment. The myth of white innocence—which, again, is another extension of white supremacist ideology—has managed, even more so than other forms of the ideology, to thrive in our so-called postracial environment because (white)[12] children are generally viewed as lacking in political, cultural, and economic consciousness and agency. Not only are they deemed innocent in this regard but they are also considered off-limits in terms of critique. This is precisely why discussions of white privilege in the news coverage of the Newtown shooting fell mostly on deaf ears and why Melissa Harris-Perry found herself in a political-medium storm when she made a rather tame joke about a family photo Mitt Romney released on twitter to introduce Kieran, a black child that his son Ben and daughter-in-law Andelynne adopted.[13]

The myth of white innocence is also difficult to identify and explode because it is insulated culturally by pervasive white sentimentality. No doubt Morrison was acutely aware of this phenomenon when she engaged the myth in *Beloved*. Indeed, the key reason that we can see the white children in the scene in *Beloved* as white supremacists-in-training is that Morrison renders them in a decidedly unsentimental way. Morrison reveals that it is precisely their innocence or conditioned white blindness to black suffering and humanity that "constitutes the crime," to borrow Baldwin's apt language. Indeed, James Baldwin usefully engages these issues of white liberal paternalism, sentimentality, and willful blindness in "Everybody's Protest Novel" when he interrogates Harriet Beecher Stowe's *Uncle Tom's Cabin* (1852) and protest fiction in general. In regard to the myth of white innocence and white liberals, his insights help elucidate how uncritical white allyship can undermine true progressive racial activism. In "Everybody's Protest Novel," he shows that, for all of her righteous indignation over the practice of slavery, Stowe, like many other white liberals of her day, was deeply invested in white supremacist ideology even as she vehemently detested chattel slavery. Given that white supremacy is parasitically dependent on a static and pathological black Other, she was faced with a rather daunting dilemma insofar as elevating her central protagonist, Uncle Tom, to hero status. Baldwin argues that Stowe resolved this ideological dilemma with Tom by "robbing" his "humanity" and "divesting" his sex. That is, in order to make the "jet-black, wooly-haired, illiterate" Uncle Tom redemptive within her white liberal paternalist framework, Stowe had to make him pathologically selfless and tether his redemption to white paternalist Christian sponsorship, protection, and logic. (Mark Twain engages in a similar, if less sophisticated, move with nigger Jim in *Huckleberry Finn*, which explains why the cruel prankster Huckleberry Finn emerges as the adult-hero and nigger Jim, who takes Finn's abuse without resentment, emerges as the child-victim in need of a white paternal messiah and rescuer.)

Invested as she was in this white paternalist Christian sponsorship, protection, and logic, Stowe could not allow Uncle Tom to have genuine sexual, emotional, psychological, and intellectual agency *and* promote white liberal paternalism as the antidote to white supremacist slavery. Consequently, Stowe characterizes Tom as emotionally incapable of harboring resentment toward his white tormentors. This thematic move is crucial as it allows white paternalist liberals to emerge as white messiahs. Indeed, they can be redeemed ethically and racially by fighting against slavery (embodied in the defenseless, childlike, loyal, and pathologically earnest Tom), while also enjoying the cultural capital of being white messiahs and having blacks forever in their debt for standing against slavery. Tom's impotence (particularly his inability to express even righteous indignation) affords white paternalistic messiahs in the novel the agency and freedom to be outraged and even violent toward other whites in defense of black victims. White messiahs stand up and in for Uncle Tom, meaning that the pathological white supremacist mindset that is chiefly responsible for creating black slavery is spared serious interrogation. In Stowe's white liberal paternalistic drama, whites swoop in and save the day and blacks play their assigned roles by suffering without malice (remember, Uncle Tom forgives even Simon Legree, who has ordered his lethal beating at the hands of other slaves, Quimbo and Sambo) and being eternally grateful to their white messiahs. Concomitantly, Tom's capital as a heroic figure depends thematically on his ability to distinguish between legitimate and illegitimate applications of white paternalism. Stowe's Tom is worthy of white liberal empathy precisely because he can make this distinction and also needs and appreciates white paternalistic intervention. Tom's willingness to forgive illegitimate applications of white paternalism is crucial too as it keeps open the possibility that *all* whites can ultimately be redeemed if they use their white entitlement/privilege to defend and protect their black charges rather than to abuse and exploit them.

Ultimately, white sentimentality obscures as much as it exposes about the problems of unchecked white domination. The key point here is that white redemption, not racial equality, is the driving motivation behind the novel. Baldwin expounds: "Sentimentality, the ostentatious parading of excessive and spurious emotion, is the mark of dishonesty, the inability to feel; the wet eyes of the sentimentalist betray his aversion to experience, his fear of life, his arid heart; and it is always, therefore, the signal of secret and violent inhumanity, the mask of cruelty."[14] Because the white act of protest is read via the white liberal paternalistic lens as magnanimous and praiseworthy, blacks are expected, if not obligated, to be grateful. The parasitical aspect of this white liberal paternalism is "forgiven . . . on the strength of . . . good intentions"[15] and regardless of the violence it unleashes on black consciousness and humanity.

Baldwin's observations about white sentimentality and paternalism are as applicable today as they were in the pre–Civil Rights era in which he made them. Indeed, the myth of white innocence embodied in the blameless and angelic white child can be usefully understood as an updated version of white sentimentality and paternalism. I refer to the myth of white innocence as "updated" because blatant expressions of white supremacy, which were commonplace prior to, and during, the Civil Rights era (Baldwin's heyday as a writer-activist), are now taboo. One could argue, in fact, that it is a lot more difficult at present to identify and challenge the myth of white innocence than in previous eras. A chief reason being that the propaganda of postraciality has taken hold with the election of the first black president, rendering suspect in the public sphere even the most legitimate claims of racialism, especially if said claims are made by people of color. Of course, postraciality is hardly a new concept, as I have explained elsewhere.[16] In fact, it predates the election of Barack Obama to the presidency by as much as a century. His presidency simply reinscribed it. The literal embodiment of a black man at the helm of the power put meat on the bones of the myth. While we're on the subject of Obama and postraciality, it bears repeating that his agency to speak truth to power about extant racial inequalities was always already limited by (white) status quo notions of humanity. Which, again, is why he was "heard" and generally applauded across political lines when he invoked the suffering of middle-class white children (as was the case with the Sandy Hook Elementary School shooting) and met with fierce resistance and controversy when he acknowledged how race informed social empathy (as was the case, especially from the political right, when he publicly linked himself to Trayvon Martin on the basis of being black, male, and subject to lethal white surveillance).

Like postraciality, the myth of white innocence constitutes another insidious way that white supremacist ideology conceals itself. The Zimmerman/Martin controversy provides a striking case in point. George Zimmerman's unconscionable stalking and slaughtering of Martin were read culturally vis-à-vis age-old racial scripts of white patriarchs defending their vulnerable charges, including not just their wives and children, but the white community at large. This is precisely why Zimmerman's legal defense team was able to turn Trayvon Martin, an innocent black teen minding his own business, into a threat deserving of lethal confrontation. In the Zimmerman/Martin scenario, Zimmerman embodied the heroic white patriarch, defending his vulnerable charges, and Martin embodied the violent black thug, whose raison d'être is to terrorize and pillage white folks. These embodied cultural scripts meant that Martin was always already the predator and Zimmerman the prey regardless of the actual facts of the case, including that Zimmerman weighed almost ninety pounds more than Martin and was bearing a loaded firearm. With the aid of draconian and thinly veiled racist laws such as Stand Your Ground Zimmerman's culpability was determined by whether he genuinely believed Martin constituted a threat. To be clear, the NRA-driven Stand Your Ground laws in Florida and elsewhere encourage (white) gun owners to not just defend themselves in the event of assault, but to actively pursue and even kill anyone they deem a threat to their person. Keep in mind, Michael Dunn, a forty-something software developer who murdered another black teen in Florida, Jordan Davis, out of malice, was initially convicted of attempted murder of Jordan's peers in the car and *not* of his actual murder of Davis. It took a second trial and the introduction of new evidence by the state prosecutor in the form of letters and phone calls in which Dunn makes explicitly racist references to blacks to finally convict him for murdering Davis. It is highly conceivable, given how the Stand Your Ground laws are written, that Dunn could have made a strong case, if not avoid jail time altogether, had he successfully murdered all the black teenagers in the car. Absurd as it may seem, the only burden of proof that is required of the person invoking the Stand Your Ground plea is that said person felt threatened at the time of ordeal. As was the case during trial, the mere perception that Martin constituted a potential threat to Zimmerman and the (white) community was the only burden the defense team needed to meet. The tenacity and social capital of these preexisting cultural scripts is precisely why the Martin family ultimately failed to re-script him in the public discourse as an innocent teenager who was racially profiled and murdered. The Martin family weren't just up against regional racial bias, but rather generations of cultural and racial scripts that depend parasitically on static notions of black immortality, hypersexuality, violence, and anti-intellectualism to maintain (white) status quo notions of normalcy. In a word, they never had a fighting chance.

The Myth of White Innocence and Entertainment

If the notions of Mammy and Uncle Tom invigorated white-messiah tropes and paternalistic white supremacy during slavery, then the updated versions of these myths in pathologically self-sacrificial, caring, and loving sidekicks, lucky charms, maids, secretaries, butlers, and mascots operate to obscure the lingering and tenacious legacy of white supremacist slavery. The myth of white innocence and attendant white sentimentality are key reasons this obscuring process is rarely engaged or contested. While there are countless examples of how this obscuring process works in the contemporary moment, I want to highlight the critically acclaimed blockbuster movie *The Green Mile*, adapted from Stephen King's novel of the same name and written and directed by Frank Darabont, and the novel *The Help* by Kathryn Stockett, which was also adapted into a blockbuster and critically acclaimed movie.

Both "texts" highlight how gender, race, sexuality, and class intersect with the myth of white innocence to naturalize black inferiority/white superiority and, by extension, extant racial inequalities. Equally as significant, both texts also enjoyed significant financial and culture support *within* black spaces, which reveals the extent to which blacks are complicit—unconsciously and consciously—in maintaining the status quo. Indeed, in 2000 Michael Clarke Duncan was nominated for an NAACP award and won a Black Reel Award in the Best Supporting Actor category for his role as death row convict and pedophile rapist John Coffey. He was also nominated for an Academy Award in 1999. In 2012 *The Help* led the way in nominations (eight) at the NAACP Image Awards Ceremony, two of which were won by Viola Davis and Octavia Spenser in the Best Actress and Supporting Actress categories for their roles as rabble rouser maids. Both actresses won Black Reel awards in their respective catego-ries as well. Finally, both were nominated for Oscar awards and Spenser won in the category of Best Supporting Actress.

In *The Green Mile*, Stephen King, who is best known for his horror novels, offers up a white nightmare in the form of a humongous black man with a seeming thirst for raping innocent white girls. The catch, so to speak, is that the white nightmare embodied in John Coffey (who was masterfully played by the 6ft. 5in. tall and 360-pound former body-guard Michael Clarke Duncan) is hardly a pedophile or thug. In fact, he is a modern-day version of Uncle Tom with the temperament and IQ of a very tame ten-year-old. Not only does he forgive the men who, like cowards, go through with his execution but he gives them the license to do so, proclaiming that he is tired of the darkness that he has witnessed in the world and looks forward to the afterlife. Consider the following conversation he has before his execution with the jailer Paul, played by Tom Hanks:

> PAUL: I have to ask you something very important now . . .
>
> JOHN: I know what ya gonna say. You don't have to say it.
>
> PAUL: No, I do. I have to say it. John, tell me what you want me to do. You want me to take you outta here? Just let you run away; see how far you could get?
>
> JOHN: Why would you do such a foolish thang?
>
> PAUL: On the Day of Judgment when I stand before God and he asks me why did I . . . did I kill one of his true miracles, what am I going to say? That it was my job? [Softly to himself] . . . that it was my job?
>
> JOHN: You tell God the father it was a kindness ya done. . . . I know ya hurtin' and worried. I can feel it on ya. But ya ought quit on, hear. I want it to be over and done wit. I do. I'm tired boss. I'm tired of being on the road, lonely as a sparrow in the rain. I'm tired of never having me a buddy to be with, to tell me where's we'ze going to, coming from, and why. . . . Most of all I'm tired of people being ugly to each other. . . . It's like pieces of glass in my head aholdin' time. Can you understand?

What prompts us to sympathize with this mountain of a man, how-ever, is not his outsized humility, but rather his inexplicable willingness to bear the sins, pain, cancer, and even responsibility of cowardly and racist white men. He, at once, shames and rejuvenates us because, like the cowardly white men in the jail who ultimately follow through with his execution despite knowing of his innocence and that the true culprit is another white man (that so happens to be in jail with John and meets his death at the hands of a virulently racist, class-privileged, and cruel jailer under the spell of John's conjuring), he never racializes his suffering or responds in a way that is appropriate to his oppression. Beyond the fact that he has been wrongly convicted and sentenced to death, he lives in a white supremacist society that routinely tortures and murders blacks to maintain social and economic dominance. Thus, it defies reason that Coffey would use his healing powers exclusively to cure and defend the very whites, and white men in particular, who are the chief enforcers of white supremacy. I say "exclusively" because, at least in the film version, we see no evidence that Coffey has used his powers to heal the group most in need of his gift: black folks suffering under the brutal thumb of white terrorism and segregation. Like *Uncle Tom's Cabin*, *The Green Mile* is not interested in seriously exploring black consciousness or subjectivity. And, it is certainly not interested in interrogating the problems of white supremacy, past or present. By all accounts, the movie is about white redemption—namely that of the Everyman, lovable racist Paul. The evil white Simon Legree-esque characters that are thrown in, Percy Wetmore and "Wild Bill" Wharton, do not complicate this narrative one bit. In fact, their presence as purely evil characters operates paradoxically to elevate Paul and the other white jailers to lovable-racist status. Because of the extreme nature of Percy and Wild Bill's racism and evil, white audiences can easily dismiss them as outliers. In relation to these outliers, Paul and his crew emerge as decent and thoughtful on matters of race and humanity even before they encounter John. By cultural extension, they are the ones that white audiences identify with—their redemption translates into the redemption of all whites.

As for the myth of white innocence, the movie does more to reinforce it via the misreading of John as a murderer-pedophile than it does to challenge it. Paul is nothing if not the embodiment of white paternalism and patriarchy. Paul's chosen profession as a jailer/policing officer also speaks metaphorically to his unspoken job of protecting the white family and community from the imagined physical threats from violence-prone, hypersexual, and white-women-lusting black men. We forgive Paul for his misreading of John, then, because as a society we remain invested in these long-standing notions of black men as thug-villains and white men as protector-saviors. Paul's initial misreading of John, like Zimmerman's alleged misreading of Martin, was "understandable" and thus forgivable given his daunting task as a white patriarch of protecting the white family and community. This narrative of white redemption only works as a pleasurable viewing experience because John is pathologically forgiving and childlike—characteristics that are all the more glaring given how received white notions of black thug-villainy are based, in part, on the imagined imposing physicality of black men, including skin tone. The bigger and blacker the man, the bigger and more urgent the threat to white safety. Had the film allowed John to have a complex adult humanity and, say, express outrage and resentment at being treated with such brutality, it is difficult to imagine the movie breaking even at the box office, let alone becoming a blockbuster. What's more, the fact that John—a black man—is willing to jeopardize his life to save those white girls and (even after being sentenced to death for a crime he didn't commit) harbors a deep resentment toward the girls' true murderer, and conjures a way to have him murdered at the hands of another white monster, legitimizes the idea that protecting white innocence is well worth dying for. We should also keep in mind that even though John is unsuccessful in protecting and saving the innocent white girls, he succeeds, via the help of Paul and his comrades, in "saving" virtuous white womanhood personified in the warden's cancer-ridden wife. To heighten the drama, of course, the director and screenwriter, Frank Darabont, eroticizes the healing encounter so as to titillate white audiences with a combination of race-sex taboo and white racial shame. We know, for instance, at this point in the film that John is not only a gentle giant and healer (of white folks) but also a sexually impotent black man. The "humor" in this scene emerges from the fact that the warden—unlike the viewers and lovable racists Paul and his crew—does not comprehend that John constitutes a tool of white paternalism and patriarchy.

Upon further reflection, we can usefully understand blacks' support of the movie in terms of their low expectations of white empathy on matters of race. Indeed, what makes *The Green Mile* instructive is its sophistication in re-presenting the pathology of white male supremacist paternalism as not only normal but noble. The re-presentation is so effective because it purports on a surface level to expose white racism as vile. But in reality the racist idea that black men in general are criminal and prone to violence is never seriously under scrutiny. In fact, just the opposite is at work. John's extreme size, "blackness," and childlike countenance mark him as a striking exception to the rule of black male criminality and violence. Our endearing feelings toward him are driven by sentimentality for his pure heart (toward whites and white children specifically), not by racial outrage about stereotyping black men as thug-villains. But, at least for the black audience, this qualified acknowledgment from whites that they are, at times, shortsighted when it comes to matters of race and racism is received as a radical gesture. The reason is clear; whites rarely acknowledge being racist or benefiting from racial oppression historically. And when they do, it tends to be apologist in nature or involve victim-blaming of one kind or another. In many ways, *The Green Mile*—with its cast of lovable racists, magical negroes, white villainous monsters, and white messiahs—constitutes the new racial formula for white redemption narratives in the twenty-first century.

Of these two award-winning movies, *The Help* seemed to generate more criticism and controversy because so many segments of black America, including the black intelligentsia, weighed in on its racial politics. Though Davis and Spenser were almost universally praised for their performances, perspectives about the racial representations of black women and white culpability in black suffering during the Civil Rights Movement differed greatly. Indeed, several highly visible celebrities and critics, such as Tavis Smiley and Nelson George, bashed the movie as whitewashing Jim Crow racism while media mogul Oprah Winfrey and the widow of slain black activist Medgar Evers (whose murder is invoked in the film), Myrlie Evers-Williams, strongly viewed it as accurately reflecting black struggle during the Civil Rights era. The black intelligentsia tended to side with the former. The Association of Black Women Historians issued an open letter repudiating the movie for trivializing the "experiences of black domestic workers."

During the 1960s, the era covered in *The Help*, legal segregation and economic inequalities limited black women's employment opportunities. Up to 90 percent of working black women in the South labored as domestic servants in white homes. *The Help's* representation of these women is a disappointing resurrection of Mammy—a mythical stereotype of black women who were compelled, either by slavery or segregation, to serve white families. Portrayed as asexual, loyal, and contented caretakers of whites, the caricature of Mammy allowed mainstream America to ignore the systemic racism that bound black women to back-breaking, low paying jobs where employers routinely exploited them. The popularity of this most recent iteration is troubling because it reveals a contemporary nostalgia for the days when a black woman could only hope to clean the White House rather than reside in it. [17]

What was telling about the controversy surrounding the movie was that few black critics or supporters of the movie mentioned the novel, which is considerably more provocative in its historical obfuscation and portrait of black women than the movie. While there are scores of examples of how the movie version of *The Help* employs a similar racial formula to *The Green Mile* to garner blockbuster status and artistic merit to boot, the novel is far more sophisticated and egregious in its execution, especially as it concerns the myth of white innocence. If *The Green Mile* movie is guilty of re-presenting white male supremacist paternalism as necessary and noble, *The Help* is guilty of a similar ideological maneuver regarding white female supremacist paternalism. Concomitantly, if John functions metaphorically in *The Green Mile* to naturalize white male supremacist paternalism and specifically the notion that white men are obligated to protect the white family from the threat of black male criminality/violence, Aibee's ideological function in the novel is to naturalize white female supremacist paternalism and specifically the notion that nurturing white mothers are the backbone of a stable white family and community at large. The rarely discussed scene in the novel in which Mae Mobley violently slaps Aibee is the most salient example of this phenomenon. Mae Mobley operates thematically as the embodiment of white innocence in the novel. Her innocence is made all the more compelling because she is neglected by her image-obsessed southern belle, racist mother Miss Leefolt, due to her chubbiness and unexceptional appearance. Even though Aibee is aware that Mae Mobley will likely turn out be like her mother as an adult, she nonetheless showers her with love and affection—essentially operating as a mammy figure/surrogate mother.

The parasitical nature of this white female supremacist paternalism and the myth of white innocence are evident in the ways that Stockett uses Aibee in this mammy-surrogate mother role to generate sympathy and empathy for Mae Mobley. In doing so, Stockett also underscores the indispensability of nurturing white motherhood. To accomplish this feat, she has to make Aibee pathologically selfless like John in *The Green Mile*. We witness this parasitical racial formula after Miss Leefolt violently spanks and scolds Mae Mobley after she yanks the phone out of her mother's hands in an effort to be acknowledged. When Aibee rushes to comfort Mae Mobley after the spanking/scolding, Mae Mobley redirects her anger at Aibee: "Mae Mobley make an ugly face at me [when I pick her up] and then rear back and *bowp*! She whack me right on the ear."[18]

Rather than express anger or even dismay about Mae Mobley's violent behavior, which leaves her "ear smarting from [Mae Mobley's] little fist,"[19] Aibee is grateful to serve as a punching bag so long as it insures Mae Mobley's safety and comfort: "I'm so glad she hit me instead a her mama, cause I don't know what that woman would a done to her. I look down and see red fingermarks on the back of her legs."[20] By having

Aibee redirect the reader's gaze from her "smarting" ear and Mae Mobley's "little fist" to the visible welts on Mae Mobley's legs, Stockett is able to generate empathy for Mae Mobley's plight and the plight of white innocence in general. Paradoxically, Aibee's pathological self-sacrificial mothering shines light on the high cultural stock of white innocence. It also operates within the discourse of white female supremacist paternalism to make Aibee a heroic figure—heroic not only because she sacrifices so freely to protect Mae Mobley and white innocence, but because she embodies what white mothering is supposed to be. Indeed, the heightened sentimentality of the scene encourages us to see Mae Mobley as the perpetual victim and her act of violence against Aibee as a trauma for Mae Mobley. As Aibee opines, had Mae Mobley directed her violence toward her mother, there's no telling "what that woman would a done."

The innocence which constitutes the crime here, to again borrow Baldwin's phrasing, is Stockett's willful white blindness to the plight and complexity of black women. She literally showers praise upon Aibee in the novel for being able to take a white punch from a toddler with a smile. The "crime," in other words, is the (strategic) erasure of working-class black women's complexity and agency in the name of loving and acknowledging them. What is being celebrated is not black women's humanity qua humanity, but rather the highly romanticized aspects of their character that supports the myth of white innocence. Though Stockett's thematic vantage point is self-consciously feminist, her parasitical rendering of black women's humanity and celebration of middle-class Victorian forms of motherhood via the myth of white innocence and updated mammy myths ultimately bankrupt the project. Rather than provide unique insights into complexities of working-class black women's lives during the pre–Civil Rights Movement—as the novel ostensibly purports to do—, it shines light on the complexities of new forms of white female supremacist paternalism.

Conclusion

In the months following the Newtown tragedy I facilitated a rather emotional class discussion in my African American studies course in Tallahassee, Florida, about the myth of white innocence and the whitewashed media coverage of the Sandy Hook Elementary School tragedy. When I surmised that had the victims been black or brown the event-wouldn't have received nearly the outpouring of social support or media coverage, several white students seemed visibly disturbed. After the class, one of them, a high-achieving senior headed to law school, approached me, disclosing that she was from Newtown and had attended Sandy Hook Elementary. While she acknowledged that race continues to play a significant role in how people are treated and viewed in society, she didn't believe that race had anything to do with the national reaction and media coverage of Sandy Hook. "They were just innocent children," she opined. "Not white or black children. *Just* children." I responded that until the day comes when black parents, such as myself, no longer have to give their sons and daughters "the talk" about how to navigate a white supremacist society that privileges the lives and experiences of white children over children of color, nobody—including those children who were brutally and senselessly murdered—is truly innocent. I further noted that as a parent and citizen I am unwilling to accept that the cultural cost of acknowledging the humanity of the children in Newtown and the unspeakable suffering their parents and community endured as a result is the erasure of black/brown children's humanity and the suffering of their parents and communities when they are senselessly killed, including by the police. I then asked her did she believe that the Sandy Hook tragedy would have received the same level of support and media coverage if the victims were black and brown and the murders had taken place on, say, the Southside of Chicago, where scores of children and young adults are, in fact, gunned down every year. She acknowledged my point, admitting that there was clearly a racial double standard in terms of which lives are worthy to mourn. Most striking about this encounter was my student's sincerity. She genuinely experienced the Newtown massacre as a "race-free" or universal tragedy even as she comprehended that all children's lives are not valued equally in our country. As the white backlash against David Sirota dramatically revealed, we have yet to reach a point in our history where we can even fully acknowledge such racial disparities in empathy, let alone have critical and constructive conversations that challenge myths of white innocence and superiority. In the final analysis, this long-standing racial reality is no less tragic than the senseless killing of little children.

THREE

"We Have More to Fear than Racism that Announces Itself": Distraction as a Strategy to Oppress

"To Whom It May Concern," I intoned. "Keep this Nigger-Boy Running."
INVISIBLE MAN BY RALPH ELLISON

The figure of the black person as threat, as criminal, as someone who is, no matter where he is going, already-on-the-way-to-prison, conditions these pre-emptive strikes [by the police], attributing lethal aggression to the very figure who suffers it most. The lives taken in this way are not lives worth grieving; they belong to the increasing number of those who are understood as ungrievable, whose lives are thought not to be worth preserving. "WHAT'S WRONG WITH 'ALL LIVES MATTER'" BY JUDITH BUTLER

Shortly after the racial debacle that allowed white police officer Darren Wilson to get away with murdering Mike Brown (at least in the eyes of most blacks), black twitter created the hashtag #iftheygunnedmedown. The goal was to call attention to the conspicuous tendency by the white plutocratic media to portray black victims visually in the most undignified ways and their white victimizers in the most humanizing ways. That is, black twitter identified a pattern in which the literal pictures of the black victims that the media chose to circulate (which were often selected from photo galleries in the victims' social media accounts) almost always tended to be ones that depicted them in the most stereotypical ways. Indeed, the media outlets would use a photo of the victim frowning, looking haggard or mock thug-posing; the visual narrative suggesting an air of criminality or violence. The portrait of the white police officer or assailant—which would typically be juxtaposed in the media frame to the black victim—would convey a radically different racial narrative. Officers were usually portrayed in professional attire, smiling, or engaged in redeeming family activities, such as opening Christmas presents or fishing with their children; the visual narrative in this instance highlighting the white individual's humanity and prompting viewers to see them in redemptive and empathetic ways.

To parody this white supremacist pattern of criminalizing black victims and decriminalizing white victimizers, black twitter protesters posted two different pictures of themselves side-by-side in a tweet—one that rendered them in attire, like tuxedos, ballroom dresses, professional uniforms, and graduation robes, that whites would likely find nonthreatening and one rendering them in attire or with facial expressions and/or hand gestures that whites would likely find threatening or "thuggish." Captions under the pictures usually reflected this political sentiment. To wit, one might read: "I wonder which one of these pictures Fox, CNN, or NBC would use in the news story #iftheygunnedmedown"? The hashtag went viral, exposing not only the extent to which our white supremacist society is hardwired to see blacks in the most negative light (especially in scenarios that involve the police or judicial system), but also the cultural collusion therein of mainstream white media outlets, including those considered "liberal" like the *New York Times* and MSNBC. More specifically, the hashtag refocused the critical lens on how the dominant culture routinely puts black victims on trial in the public domain whenever they are assaulted or killed by the police or other representatives of dominant (white) power. This pattern of victim blaming inevitably places the onus on victimized black communities to prove to the white-dominated news and media outlets, criminal justice system, and general public that black victims are not guilty of provoking the violence perpetuated against them. This pattern of perpetually placing blacks in this defensive posture is immensely advantageous to the dominant white supremacist power structure as it allows whites to blame imagined black pathologies for black social and economic struggles without having to contend with their white privilege, pathological racist behavior or the white supremacist power structure that licenses black social degradation and death. As we have witnessed time and again, this pattern of victim blaming has proven quite effective, including when the victims were unarmed children (Trayvon Martin, Tamir Rice, and Jordan Davis); unarmed shoppers or people in need of assistance after car trouble or accidents (John Crawford, Renisha McBride, Jonathan Ferrell, and Corey Jones); people involved in minor infractions (Freddie Gray, Laquan McDonald, and Eric Garner); or people defending themselves against physically and/or verbally abusive cops (Mike Brown and Sandra Bland).

In this chapter I will engage this long-standing pattern of victim blaming and the challenges it poses in the twenty-first century for asserting black humanity and acquiring justice and equal treatment under the law. I will refer to this pattern of victim blaming and related forms of displacing blame for white supremacist oppression onto blacks as the "discourse of racial distraction." Further, I will consider the ways that blacks have (unwittingly) dignified or reinforced this discourse and, conversely, the ways that blacks have successfully exposed and exploded it. Toni Morrison's insights on racism as a distraction tactic offers a useful starting point for understanding the social, cultural, and economic implications of this phenomenon for blacks. Morrison argues that racism is designed ideologically to keep blacks forever bogged down emotionally, culturally, and intellectually in trying to prove their humanness to their white oppressors:

The very serious function of racism . . . is distraction. It keeps you from doing your work. It keeps you explaining, over and over again, your reason for being. Somebody says you have no language, so you spend twenty years proving that you do. Somebody says your head isn't shaped properly, so you have scientists working on the fact that it is. Someone says you have no art, so you dredge that up. Somebody says you have no kingdoms, so you dredge that up. None of that is necessary. There will always be one more thing.[1]

What she refers to as a "distraction" is indeed a key function of white supremacist ideology—to hold blacks chiefly responsible for their extant victimization from slavery to present-day institutional racism and structural inequalities: the chief goal being to keep blacks preoccupied with defending their humanity to whites and, by turn, focused on how blacks contribute to their own oppression rather than on how the social and material realities of white supremacist oppression—past and present—undermines and sabotages black progress and self-determination. Paradoxically, the preoccupation with proving their humanity to whites legitimizes white supremacy as it places them in the privileged position of determining black humanity. Because their white privilege depends on denying their history of oppressing blacks and, specifically, how whites continue to reap the social and economic benefits of this history of oppression, they have a deeply vested interest in keeping blacks in this defensive ideological posture. Which is also, consequently, why blacks who emphasize black culpability in oppression to the exclusion of historic white oppression, such as Ward Connelly, Clarence Thomas, Bill Cosby, Charles Barkley, and Don Lemon, become white media darlings and are often treated as brave and heroic for being willing to "call blacks out" for their social and economic woes.

In a pragmatic sense, it is useful to think of the discourse of distraction as a long-standing apparatus of white supremacist ideology designed ostensibly to misunderstand black Americans' plight and, by extension, trivialize whites' culpability in blacks' subordinate social, cultural, and economic status. As we will discuss shortly, this intentional misunderstanding gave way in more contemporary times to a culture of conditioned ignorance, encouraging whites to experience this distraction maneuver as commonsensical and, conversely, blacks' challenges to it as frivolous, even racist. We can trace this phenomenon of intentional misunderstanding back to slavery. Proslavery whites experienced the atrocity of slavery during the antebellum era as a civilizing apparatus for enslaved Africans. That is, enslavement was understood or, rather, strategically misunderstood as a benefit to Africans as it not only "saved" them from their "primitive" existence in Africa but also "exposed" them to white Western civilization and most importantly (white) Christianity. White slavers situated themselves as paternal figures ordained by God who were responsible for the care and discipline of the enslaved. The enslaved Africans were prefigured in this white supremacist paternalist calculus as perpetually childlike in their understanding of morality, civilization, work ethic, and self-determination and in need of constant instruction, surveillance, and discipline. Manual labor in this context was a way for the enslaved to "earn their keep" while at the same time providing them with exposure to white civilization and paths beyond their imagined primitive nature and pathological cultures. In keeping with this mindset, white paternalism was necessarily violent at times because the enslaved, especially the men, were considered violent, hypersexual, and immoral by nature. White violence against enslaved blacks was thus experienced—emotionally, legally, and religiously—as either paternalistic discipline or a form of self-defense. Of course, white lethal violence against blacks spiked dramatically after slavery was abolished and the subsequent failure of Reconstruction because whites, especially in the South, no longer had an economic incentive to protect their "property." Slave labor was expensive and chiefly the economic domain of the wealthy. Thus employing lethal force was a path of last resort. Dead slaves were wasted capital.

Despite the widely held belief that the enslaved Africans were intellectually, socially, and morally inferior, laws were passed that made it illegal to teach them to read and write. Indeed, treating the enslaved as equals was strongly discouraged and even punishable by law. The goal was to establish a culture of white supremacy/black inferiority in concert with state-sanctioned violence to keep the enslaved, at once, intimidated and in fear of white supremacist power but also dependent on the white supremacist culture to determine their social value and even divinity (or lack thereof). Though to a degree the enslaved were treated as animals insofar as how they were bought, sold, and traded, they were held to a higher moral standard than whites—a standard, however, that only recognized their human agency to the degree to which they could transgress the white supremacist moral code. What we know from Thomas Jefferson's failed attempt to include blacks as citizens in the "Declaration of Independence" (along with a statement condemning King George for trying to rally blacks to fight for the British in the Revolutionary War in exchange for freedom) is that our white founding fathers were well aware of the contradiction between fighting for self-determination and liberty against British tyranny and keeping blacks enslaved in the new republic.

In *Silent Covenants* Derrick Bell speaks directly to this issue of intentional misunderstanding as it concerned white dealings with newly freed blacks in the post-Reconstruction era. He argues that since that era white individuals' "sense of self" has been tied to the "set of [racialized] assumptions, privileges, and benefits that accompany the status of being white."[2] These assumptions, privileges, and benefits have over time become valuable assets that "whites seek to protect."[3] Even though there were salient physical markers in the post-Reconstruction era that reinforced these "assets" like segregated public facilities and black disenfranchisement, whites (especially in the middle and lower classes) needed the added physical display of power over a largely defenseless black population to truly feel privileged. The white elite encouraged this racial thinking as it distracted the masses from how they were coercing and manipulating them in the name of free market economy. By scapegoating blacks as the primary threat to white self-determination and the pursuit of the American Dream, the white elite was able to galvanize the white masses around a common enemy. Instead of providing the masses with access to real wealth and power, they provided them with embodied wealth in the form of control and dominance over blacks. Bell surmises that white expressions of racial hate in the form of physical intimidation and lynching "had its roots in an unconscious realization that the property rights in whiteness had *real meaning* only as defenseless Negroes were terrorized and murdered."[4] Not only does Bell's theory explain why black assertions of humanity and demands for equality continue to be mischaracterized by whites as hostile and antiwhite (consider the resistance to the Black Lives Matter movement across the political spectrum), but it also explains why whites see expressions of these property rights—like the police killings of unarmed blacks—as justifiable, if not emotionally soothing. To a large degree, this phenomenon also explains why a billionaire like Donald Trump with a long track record of lying and hustling the white poor and middle class was able to convince them via a political campaign premised on race baiting, Islamophobia, and xenophobia to vote against their best economic and social interests and elect him to the presidency.

Morrison's depiction in *Beloved* of how whites displaced their racial violence onto enslaved blacks sheds additional light on the ideological roots of racial distraction and further elucidates why exposing and exploding such distraction is a steep and daunting challenge for blacks:

White people believed that whatever the manners, under every dark skin was a jungle. Swift unnavigable waters, swinging screaming baboons, sleeping snakes, red gums ready for their sweet white blood. In a way . . . they were right. The more coloredpeople spent their strength trying to convince them how gentle they were, how clever and loving, how human, the more they used themselves up to persuade whites of something Negroes believed could not be questioned, the deeper and more tangled the jungle grew inside. But it wasn't the jungle blacks brought with them to this place from the other (livable) place. It was the jungle whitefolks planted in them. And it grew. It spread. In, through and after life, it spread, until it invaded the whites who had made it. Touched them every one. Changed and altered them. Made them bloody, silly, worse than even they wanted to be, so scared were they of the jungle they had made. The screaming baboon lived under their own white skin; the red gums were their own.[5]

Here, Morrison delineates the distraction of racism as an infectious disease that corrupts white and black consciousness alike. For blacks, the disease of distraction intensifies the more they try to convince whites of their humanness; that they have transcended the primitiveness of their African roots and cultural heritage. The rub is that the notions of African primitivism/European civilization and, concomitantly, of whites saving Africans from a primitive existence are premised upon white supremacy. As Morrison's narrator explains above, the so-called jungle of Africa is the "livable" space for blacks and the imagined space of civilization in the United States is the true barbarous space. Fighting for white acceptance is thus unhealthy and even traumatizing for blacks as it requires appealing to the very perpetrators of slavery, black death, violence, and trauma for human recognition. Because race is, at bottom, a social fiction, whites' dehumanizing behavior toward blacks has serious repercussions for their own humanity. That is to say, by devaluing black life in this way they are ultimately devaluing their own. Indeed, they become in their treatment of blacks the very savages and barbarians that they imagine Africans to be.

Historically speaking, Frederick Douglass's iconic speech "What to the Slave is the Fourth of July" in 1852 is arguably the most brilliant interrogation of how this racial displacement operated during slavery to trivialize black suffering. Equally as important, he illuminates the major stakes that even antislavery whites had in preserving and defending aspects of what Bell calls white property rights. Addressing an abolitionist women's group during an Independence Day celebratory event, he explains how white supremacist thinking informs and corrupts even antislavery white liberal appeals. He argues, for example, that aggressive political agitation and even radical acts of civil unrest, such as the Boston Tea Party, are far more effective than appeals to (white) reason and white moral decency because the latter presumes that white ignorance and misunderstanding drives white support of slavery rather than willful blindness.

But I fancy I hear some one of my audience say, it is just in this circumstance that you and your brother abolitionists fail to make a favorable impression on the public mind. Would you argue more, and denounce less, would you persuade more, and rebuke less, your cause would be much more likely to succeed. But, I submit, where all is plain there is nothing to be argued. What point in the anti-slavery creed would you have me argue? On what branch of the subject do the people of this country need light? Must I undertake to prove that the slave is a man? That point is conceded already. Nobody doubts it. The slaveholders themselves acknowledge it in the enactment of laws for their government. They acknowledge it when they punish disobedience on the part of the slave. There are seventy-two crimes in the State of Virginia, which, if committed by a black man, (no matter how ignorant he be), subject him to the punishment of death; while only two of the same crimes will subject a white man to the like punishment. What is this but the acknowledgement that the slave is a moral, intellectual and responsible being?[6]

Douglass recognizes that appeals to white reason and morality constitute a "distraction," and a parasitical one at that, because they place the onus on blacks to demonstrate they are not inherently inferior and pathological. As Douglass so deftly points out, the awareness of black humanity is not only written into the law but structured in such a way as to hold blacks to a higher moral standing than whites. So whites recognize black humanity and agency only to the extent to which it benefits them socially, culturally, religiously, and economically to do so. What the laws demonstrate, then, is that misunderstanding blacks' humanity and plight is a key ideological component to justifying their enslavement. The white liberal response of appealing to white reason and morality is thus hardly revolutionary as it places the onus on blacks to prove to whites what they already know to be true and have a significant socioeconomic stake in *not* knowing or acknowledging—namely, that blacks are human beings whose basic rights to freedom have been ruthlessly trampled on by whites for economic, social, and cultural gain. What is particularly striking here is Douglass's tone of indignation at even having to make the case that blacks are humans. He rightly sees the white liberals' proposed mode of argumentation as the racial distraction that it is. Any fool can distinguish between a man and a dog. Expecting him to do so is the height of insult, especially considering that he has been invited to speak in celebration of Independence Day—a holiday designed to honor white revolutionaries who were once classified as outlaws and traitors by the British Empire. Indeed, he points out that the heroes of the Revolutionary War believed that self-determination and democracy were non-negotiable and they were willing to die to secure them. To demand the enslaved be patient in the wake of an even more egregious form of imperialism is beyond hypocritical. Douglass was having none of it. He demands that those who claim to be on the side of justice and liberty for enslaved Africans be as vehement in their antislavery protest as the celebrated figures of the Revolutionary War were against imperialist British rule.

Like Douglass before her, Morrison is acutely aware that the white supremacist game of determining blacks' human agency—past and present—is rigged; that what counts as a legitimate human response for whites does not necessarily apply to blacks. Morrison embodies this dynamic again in *Beloved* when Sixo kills a shoat to eat. When the white master schoolteacher accuses him of stealing the shoat, Sixo cunningly responds that he was "improving your property, sir."[7] He then elaborates, "Sixo plant rye to give the high piece a better chance. Sixo take and feed the soil, give you more crop. Sixo give you more work."[8] Here,

Sixo cracks the code of provisional humanity extended to the enslaved during slavery. We clearly witness that the only legitimate agency that Sixo possesses is the agency to break the law/moral code. When he flips the white supremacist slavery script and uses his legal status as property to expose and explode the calculus of provisional humanity he is predictably whipped. Indeed, schoolteacher resorted to violence to reinforce the idea that "that definitions belong to the definers—not the defined."[9]

We see this definer-defined phenomenon of power and distraction most dramatically in our current racial discourse around lethal (white) policing of black/brown communities in the ways that many whites and the white-dominated plutocratic media fixate on fringe looters and vandals rather than on the racialist police culture and the undeniable historical pattern of excessive force and brutality against black citizens. James Baldwin engages this phenomenon brilliantly in a 1968 interview with *Esquire Magazine* shortly after Martin Luther King Jr.'s assassination. When the smug white *Esquire* interviewer tries to hold "black looters" responsible, in part, for the brutal response of the white police force to protest marches, Baldwin avers,

How would you define somebody who puts a cat where he is and takes all the money out of the ghetto where he makes it? Who is looting whom? Grabbing off [sic] the TV set? He doesn't really want the TV set. He's saying screw you. It's just judgment, by the way, on the value of the TV set. He doesn't want it. He wants to let you know he's there. The question I'm trying to raise is a very serious question. The mass media-television and all the major news agencies endlessly use that word "looter". On television you always see black hands reaching in, you know. And so the American public concludes that these savages are trying to steal everything from us. And no one has seriously tried to get where the trouble is. After all, you're accusing a captive population who has been robbed of everything of looting. I think it's obscene.[10]

Here, Baldwin astutely dodges the distraction trap, as it were, of treating violent black responses to white violence as the source of the racial conflict. What he points out as "obscene" is the audacity of the chief historical white perpetrators of looting and violence against black humanity to proclaim that they are somehow victims when blacks retaliate in self-defense or protest against such white assaults. Indeed, Baldwin identifies and exposes the ways in which the white journalist is racializing looting and violence as if white rage and lethal violence against black struggle for civil rights and structural equality is rational and black rage against white racism and institutionalized inequality is misplaced, if not pathological. As Carol Anderson rightly notes, "White rage doesn't have to take to the streets and face rubber bullets to be heard. Instead, white rage carries an aura of respectability and has access to the courts, police, legislatures and governors, who cast its efforts as noble, though they are actually driven by the most ignoble motivations."[11] To Baldwin's point, white rage against black progress is really the driving force behind black/white racial conflict in the United States and the police force is just one of several mediums—including the judicial and prison systems, state and federal governments, and corporate America—that enforce and perpetuate it. As he was so politically adept at doing, Baldwin turns the table on white supremacist tactics of distraction by focusing on the pathological nature of white racial logic. More specifically, he identifies as pathological the white habit of perpetually blaming blacks for the consequences of long-standing patterns of white oppression and then claiming ignorance and innocence when their destructive tactics breed civil unrest and protest like the Civil Rights and Black Power movements. He opines,

Your history [of delusional racist thinking and behavior] has led you to this moment [of civil unrest and protest], and you can only begin to change yourself by looking at what you are doing in the name of your history, in the name of your gods, in the name of your language. And what has happened is as though I . . . can see it [the problem] better than you can see it. Because I cannot afford to let you fool me. If I let you fool me, then I die. But I've fooled *you* for a long time. That's why you keep saying, what does the Negro want? It's a summation of your own delusions, the lies you've told yourself. You know *exactly* what I want!

What Baldwin is speaking to are the paradoxical ways in which white supremacist ideology allows whites to avoid confronting what they already know but refuse to contend with about white power. The dye was cast, so to speak, during slavery when slave owners would routinely ask their slaves if they were satisfied. The goal of this questioning was never to get a true assessment of how the enslaved actually felt about their deplorable conditions, but rather to ease their conscience about their inhumanity against the enslaved by having the enslaved vocalize and confirm their satisfaction about their condition, if not gratitude for being "rescued" from the supposed savagery of Africa. In other words, the goal of the theater of questioning was to perpetuate a lie of white supremacist slavery—a lie that was sustained legally and otherwise by making sure that the enslaved were denied access to education, legal recourse, self-determination, and, of course, guns. As Frederick Douglass explains in *The Narrative*, it was understood among the slaves that one was never to tell a slave master the truth. Indeed, doing so was akin to committing suicide as a disgruntled slave, especially a male, was a threat to not only run away, which was a costly affair, but also to foment insurrection. This white supremacist pattern of orchestrating blacks to lie or, at least, soft peddle the racial realities of their circumstances persist to this day, albeit in less obvious forms.

Racial Distraction, #BlackLivesMatter, and Resistance Politics

Critiques of this white supremacist pattern of orchestrated ignorance about white oppression are crucial as they demonstrate how distraction always already bankrupts productive dialogue across racial lines. As Douglass's speech dramatically demonstrates, whites have always known blacks want (at the very least) true freedom, equal protection under the law, socioeconomic prosperity, and cultural respectability as American citizens. The problem—then as now—is that giving blacks what they want comes at the dangerous risk of jeopardizing white power and dominance. Indeed, the most pressing question for a majority of whites on this racial front in the current era is why are blacks so angry and demanding, considering how much material and cultural benefits of white supremacy whites have already conceded. In fact, white racial entitlement is so bound up to how whites experience self-determination, individual agency, and liberation that a majority of whites believe erroneously that whites are the most oppressed group in the United States. It is clear from the way that Black Lives Matter protestors are engaging with mainstream media outlets and politicians that they are acutely aware of this discourse of distraction and working aggressively to expose and upend it.

Though there are countless examples of this dynamic (including how the movement has utilized social media to expose journalistic bias when reporting on blue-on-black murder and brutality), the moment that stands out most to my mind is when BLM activist DeRay McKesson obliterated CNN journalist Wolf Blitzer's discourse of distraction on national TV when discussing the Baltimore uprising. Rather than focus on the problems of white supremacist policing that led to the brutal murder of Freddie Gray, which ignited the uprising, Blitzer displaces the blame of Gray's death and, by extension, the hyperpolicing of black youth onto poor black communities and particularly "thuggish" black male youth. Indeed, he makes a thinly veiled argument that the black public outcry over Gray's murder—some of it resulting in property damage—undermines the political message of BLM and explains, if not justifies, why aggressive police tactics are warranted and necessary. Employing whitewashed quotes from Martin Luther King Jr. about non-violent protest and rebukes from President Obama about looting and property damage, Blitzer tries rhetorically to strong-arm McKesson into discrediting, not only the violent protestors, but the entire movement against the Baltimore police. After citing King for racial leverage, Blitzer asks McKesson if he supports peaceful protests. Recognizing Blitzer's tactic of white supremacist distraction, McKesson responds: "Yes, for sure [I want peaceful protest]. Remember the people who have been violent since August have been the police. We think [sic] about the 300 people that have been killed this year alone. That is violence. There has been property damage here that's been really unfortunate. . . . But remember there have been many days of peaceful protests in Baltimore and places all around the country." Undeterred, Blitzer asks McKesson if he agrees with President Obama that there is "no excuse for the violence, stealing and arson."[12] McKesson fires back, "Pain manifests in different ways and I don't have to condone it to understand it. People are grieving and mourning. But they also know that Freddie Gray will never be back and those windows will be." Finally, when Blitzer says that the violence is "distracting from the peaceful protests" and goes directly against the wishes of the Gray family, McKesson avers: "Distraction from progress is when city officials get on TV and call black people in pain thugs—that's a distraction. The unrest and the uprising . . . is a cry for justice here and across the country because the police continue to terrorize people. . . . Broken windows are not broken spines. People are in pain." Directly addressing President Obama's rebuke, he concludes, "I hope [the president] understands the conditions that created the unrest . . . because Freddie Gray will never see another day."[13]

Considering that Blitzer invoked King to discredit violent uprising, it is worth noting that in 1966 when King was pressed by white journalist Mike Wallace to denounce the Black Power movement and so-called riots it incited, King responded thoughtfully that "a riot is the language of the unheard."[14] What King clearly understood (and indeed what BLM activists like McKesson are building on and carrying forward politically) is that such questions are politically and racially loaded—Wallace was displacing blame for white violence and oppression onto blacks. King sidesteps the ideological "trap" of pathologizing blackness by highlighting white blindness and making clear that black outrage, even of a violent sort, is understandable to the degree to which black people are being oppressed and brutalized by whites with impunity. Similarly, McKesson does not accommodate Blitzer's discourse of distraction. Instead, he challenges the ideological underpinnings of the questions. When Blitzer tries to key in on the problems of looting and property damage, McKesson refocuses the debate on black human suffering and the structural problems (like corrupt and racially biased police forces and racially tone-deaf politicians) that foment unrest in Baltimore and across the country. What he makes clear, like King before him, is that looting and property damage are symptoms rather than the disease of racial and structural inequalities. The rub is that Blitzer and Wallace perform in their questioning of McKesson and King precisely the kind of distraction tactics and white erasures of black suffering that provoke black uprisings.

Of course the more potent forms of resistance to this discourse of distraction emerge in the form of collective economic protest such as occurred at the University of Missouri in 2015, resulting in the forced resignation of university president Tim Wolfe. What often happens, however, is that the white supremacist power structure adapts and adjusts when tactics of distraction do not succeed in pacifying black protests.[15] The National Basketball Association's (NBA's) averted racial crisis in 2014 comes readily to mind. When Adam Silver banned Clipper owner Donald Sterling from the league during the NBA playoffs after recordings of his racist rants against black people and NBA stars surfaced, he was roundly praised, including by many black NBA players. The socioeconomic reality, however, was that Silver had very little choice but to act as he did because anything short of banning Sterling from the league was bound to ignite a black player revolt. The National Basketball Player Association's vice president, Roger Mason Jr., was on record saying that a boycott of the NBA playoffs was all but inevitable had Silver not banned Sterling. What Silver accomplished was hardly seismic in terms of changing the racially problematic culture of the nearly all white male ownership. Sterling was merely the fall guy of the moment; the one who was caught saying what likely most of the other owners felt about black players and patrons. Indeed, Sterling intimated as much in several open threats to expose other owners with similar views. Silver's actions then just assuaged the racial tensions of the moment. White patriarchal capitalist power didn't get obliterated; it merely adjusted itself to maintain dominance. And, by all counts, it worked. Another white male billionaire, Steve Ballmer, purchased the Clippers at a premium price. In turn, Sterling made millions of dollars on the sale and the NBA finals proceeded as scheduled. We can read Silver's move as another form of distraction because it strategically *misidentified* Sterling as the culprit rather than the white capitalist supremacist culture of the NBA.

The culture of distraction is so much a part of our racial discourse that often even blacks who recognize racism as a serious problem reify it. The push by many prominent, self-proclaimed black leaders for police officers to wear body cameras, as if doing so will strongly deter racial violence, is a striking case in point. While the paucity of data on the effectiveness of body cameras to reduce instances of police interactions makes it inconclusive at best, there's ample historical evidence to demonstrate that having visual proof of police abuse and misconduct is not sufficient to prevent lethal police interactions with black communities. Rodney King's brutal beating in 1991 at the hands of white cops was caught on tape, as was Eric Garner's homicide. The outcome in both cases was that no police officers were prosecuted, at least not at the state level.[16]

To be clear, I am not suggesting that body cameras are useless or that those blacks who endorse them are willfully complicit in racial distraction (Michael Brown's parents also strongly endorse the idea), but, rather, that it is naïve and dangerous to think that we can resolve longstanding patterns of abusive white policing by placing cameras on police officers and in squad cars. What we are ultimately fighting is a culture of white supremacy within police departments that largely reflects the culture of white supremacy in our society. It is hardly a stretch to say that most whites would not see a problem with the fact that Ferguson, which is 70 percent African American, has a police department that is more than 90 percent white (fifty of the fifty-three officers are white), a white mayor (who apparently thinks that there are virtually no racial tensions in Ferguson), and a nearly all-white city council. As we have witnessed time and again, the nearly all-white Ferguson police department and governing body (the overwhelming majority of whom live in predominantly white sections of Ferguson or in neighboring white communities) have little respect or understanding toward the African American community. While some of these whites no doubt harbor racist attitudes, I suspect many do not—at least not consciously. Which is to say that I strongly suspect that only a few of these whites are overtly racist in their dealings with blacks. Or, put another way, the majority of these whites do not experience their racist behaviors toward blacks as racist because of internalized and institutionalized white supremacy.

Eduardo Bonilla-Silva coined the term "color-blind racism" to identify this phenomenon of practicing or benefiting from racism without being actively or consciously racist. He cautions against an empowerment strategy of trying to assess how many whites "hate or love blacks and other minorities" because it distracts us from the pervasiveness of white supremacy and the participation therein by "good white folks." As Morrison avers in *Playing in the Dark*, white self-hood is parasitically dependent upon black economic, social, and cultural inferiority; thus, reproducing and policing white supremacy in myriad forms are fundamental to white identity and consciousness. Focusing on white intent is counterproductive, then, as it woefully underestimates how intensely normative white identity depends on keeping blacks in subordinate social, economic, and cultural status. As Robin DiAngelo reminds us, many whites who are overtly antiracist in their racial politics are nevertheless fiercely protective of white privilege. Which explains why even the slightest challenge, especially by blacks, to their notions of themselves as "good white folks" triggers defensive responses.

Again the problem is not that we lack proof of police misconduct and simply need more substantive evidence; the problem is that in a white supremacist society white feelings of racial insecurity and racial bias have serious political currency and indeed often trump actual facts. Keep in mind, that virtually all the cases that have generated national and international attention of late involve armed whites instigating confrontation with unarmed black men/boys and then later claiming self-defense when these confrontations result in the death of their assailants. The harsh racial reality is that the claim of fearing black violence and thuggery—however irrationally presented or explained—has tremendous currency in a white supremacist environment.

And here it is important to identify the irrational white fear of black men as a social invention and demonstrate how it embodies the distraction of racism. As many scholars have pointed out, black on black crime (which is often cited by many whites and even some blacks as proof that blacks are inherently pathological and have only themselves to blame for their heightened police surveillance and aggressiveness) is not some unique phenomenon of criminality and violence that negatively sets blacks apart from whites and other racial groups. Whites commit crimes against other whites at roughly the same rates that blacks commit crimes against other blacks—hovering around 90 percent for the past decade at least. And this pattern of *intra*racial crime makes perfect sense considering that criminals tend to commit crimes in their neighborhoods and against folks who tend to look like them. Moreover, what we also know is that only about 5 percent of the black population is responsible for the overwhelming majority of crimes. Which is another way of saying that 95 percent of black Americans are law-abiding citizens. Lest we forget too, in 1982 Ronald Reagan's so-called War on Drugs (which George Bush Sr. and Bill Clinton later intensified) manufactured a new black criminal—that is, a criminal in the form of a low-end (black) drug user. Though whites use drugs at roughly the same rate as blacks, blacks were the chief losers of this political agenda by design. Indeed, Reagan launched this agenda when less than 2 percent of the population felt that drug usage was a major social problem. As Ian Haney López notes in *Dog Whistle Politics*, the goal of Reagan's campaign was to shift the national focus away from white collar crimes to petty crimes—a move which galvanized the white masses against blacks instead of the white elite, who posed by far the most serious economic threat to the white masses.[17] Even more insidious, Reagan helped facilitate the mass influx of cocaine to the United States to support his illegal war in Nicaragua against the Sandinista guerillas who overthrew the brutal dictator and US ally Anastasio Somoza in 1979. When Congress refused to support Reagan's idea to fund the Contras—a guerilla group comprised of former Somoza loyalists—he conspired with the Contras to fund their war against the Sandinistas via drug money; the main clients were United States citizens and especially poor blacks in urban spaces. To accomplish this illegal feat he employed the CIA to relax enforcement of drug trafficking into the United States. Reagan's self-made drug crisis had the perfect cover in blaming African Americans because most whites—then and now—are predisposed to seeing blacks as immoral and prone to criminality.[18] As a direct result of federal and state law changes regarding drug usage stemming from the War on Drugs, the prison population exploded; between 1980 and 2000 there was a 1,100 percent increase.[19] Tellingly, the bulk of those incarcerated under these new laws were marijuana users instead of the drug lords or hard drugs users that state and federal governments with the aid of mainstream media have perpetuated as the real targets of such legislation.

Blacks have been most damaged by the War on Drugs because they are disproportionately poor (meaning that they had to rely on overwhelmed and understaffed court-appointed attorneys to defend them or none at all)[20] and the policing and judicial systems are biased in favor of whites (especially those with expendable capital). The fact that marijuana has now become all but legalized across the country throws this reality of racially biased policing and judiciary practices radically into focus. The very drug responsible for filling the prisons with recreational black drug users is now being sold legally to a mostly white middle-class clientele by mostly white capitalists and will likely generate billions of dollars in tax revenues for participating states over the coming years.

Erstwhile, there has been little political movement (beyond some conveniently timed, election-cycle speeches about prison reform by President Obama and former presidential candidate Hillary Clinton) to free the millions of mostly black prisoners who have been imprisoned (some of them for decades) for what is now essentially legal.

Crucial to note here is that whites tend to favor laws that disproportionately disadvantage blacks. Scholars Mark Peffley and Jon Hurwitz discovered this trend when researching racial attitudes about the death penalty. In the study, they first asked blacks and whites about their support of the death penalty (which they used as their baseline condition) and then surveyed them with two separate argument prompts, the first being that "the death penalty is unfair because too many innocent people are being executed" and the second being that "the death penalty is unfair because most people who are executed are African Americans." Per their expectations, blacks' views of the death penalty became significantly negative after being presented with both arguments; the drop was 16 percent after hearing the first argument and 12 percent after hearing the second. In stark contrast, white support remained virtually unchanged when presented with the first argument but skyrocketed to a 12 percent increase when presented with the second argument—an outcome that stunned the researchers.[21] They conclude, "whites overall not only reject the racial argument against the death penalty, but some move strongly in the direction *opposite* to the argument. For example, whereas 36% of whites strongly favor the death penalty in the baseline condition (where they were just asked whether they supported it), 52% strongly favor it when presented with the argument that the policy is racially unfair." This trend substantiates Derrick Bell's argument about whiteness as a property right; whites support racially biased laws because they increase the cultural capital of whiteness. The frightening reality this study forecasts is that white support for blue-on-black police killings will likely increase rather than decrease because of the added publicity that such incidents are receiving nationally.

Why Respectability Will Not Save Us

Prior to the Civil Rights Movement whites would often tell a black person who they felt was exceptional in some way that they "were a credit to their race." This "compliment" was premised on the idea that blacks were inherently inferior to whites and fueled the distraction mindset that the path to equality was not about exploding white supremacy but eradicating the destructive mindsets within black spaces. This racial calculus treated white supremacy/black inferiority as normative. Moreover, it perpetuated the Horatio Alger myth of American meritocracy and rugged self-determination. What we know, however, is that individuality and self-determination are reserved culturally for whites only, especially those with substantial economic resources. Indeed, being white in a white supremacist culture means getting the benefit of the doubt whenever one's behavior and/or achievement falls short of cultural expectations and, concomitantly, being viewed as racially normative when one excels in either or both categories. Which explains why white mass murderers/domestic terrorists like Adam Lanza, James Holmes, Dylann Roof, and Robert Lewis Dear were humanized in the media and the public domain despite their heinous acts.

In the *Charlotte Observer* white Shelby police chief Jeff Ledford described Roof (who callously murdered nine African Americans in a church to ignite a race war and displayed no remorse and expressed "racist views" during his arrest) as "very quiet" and "not problematic."[22] In a stunning display of white privilege, Roof received a meal from Burger King shortly after he told arresting officers he was hungry. The white judge who arraigned Roof, Magistrate James Gosnell Jr., opened the court proceedings by imploring the black families of the murdered victims to see Roof's family as "victims" also who need consideration and help. It was later revealed that Gosnell had once been reprimanded in 2003 for using the epithet "nigger" in court to describe blacks.[23] Dear (who murdered three people, including a white police officer, and wounded nine others) was initially described in the *New York Times* as a "gentle loner who occasionally unleashed violent acts towards neighbors and women he knew."[24] The highly respected newspaper also treated as legitimate the widely debunked videos suggesting that Planned Parenthood sold baby parts which Dear invoked after his arrest as the catalyst for his terrorist assault on the women's health organization.[25] Police unions across the country which have been outspoken about the so-called "Ferguson Effect"[26]—a now-disproven link between antipolice violence and the Black Lives Matter protests—were conspicuously silent about Dear's cop killing and its political linkages. It also bears noting that Holmes, Roof,[27] and Dear were all taken into custody with nary a scratch on them.

In stark contrast to the treatment of white individuality and self-determination as normative within this racial calculus, blacks are viewed monolithically as inferior and always measured against the most unfavorable individuals among its ranks. Individuality of the kind that whites routinely enjoy is nonexistent. The black individual that defies stereotypes—which is to say the overwhelming majority of blacks—is perpetually treated as the exception to the rule of black pathology and inferiority. Then as now, blacks deemed a "credit to their race" (or "exceptional" in modern-day parlance) were those who somehow managed to rise above this status quo pathology and inferiority. For the better part of the twentieth century whites enforced this mindset with orchestrated terrorism, routinely using law enforcement and the justice system in general as weapons. When, say, a black person broke a social, cultural, or economic boundary set by whites (typically designed to keep the latter in power), the whites attacked the entire community, not just the offending agent. The goal of punishing and terrorizing the entire community for the nonconforming acts of an individual was to promote fear and encourage blacks to police each other into accommodating white supremacist law and order. (Leaving Mike Brown's corpse in full display under the sweltering sun for nearly five hours is the modern-day version of this practice.) The lie about racial equality that this white supremacist mindset perpetuated was that white fear and violence toward blacks was a direct result of black criminality and hyperviolence. To change this calculus (i.e., to make whites less afraid of and more accepting of blacks as equals) meant that blacks had to take responsibility for white fear, anxiety, and anger. It bears repeating that black respectability politics was developed around this racial mindset of distraction. This entailed exhausting energy and resources trying to prove to whites that most blacks were closer to whites in terms of their intellect, moral character, and work ethic and should not be viewed in the same negative light as the depraved and criminal-minded minority within their ranks. This black preoccupation with proving their worth to whites was a white supremacist distraction tactic to the degree to which it encouraged blacks to be hypercritical of their behavior and hyperforgiving of white terrorism and oppression. The reality was that white terrorism and violence were employed to maintain white dominance over black communities. Racial equality was—and continues to be—a threat to whites for obvious reasons. The more blacks and people of color are given equal opportunity and access to power, the more unearned racial privilege whites have to give up. That is precisely why largely symbolic successes like electing the first black president to two terms seem to have intensified rather than ameliorated racial tensions in this country. The white supremacist distraction politics of old ensconced the agenda of maintaining white supremacy in rhetoric about personal responsibility, protecting white womanhood, and rampant black criminality. Respectability politics as a strategy for racial uplift was doomed from the outset because it was premised on an orchestrated lie—that whites were so mistrusting of and violent toward blacks because of black criminality, corruption, and violence. The truth was that whites were the true culprits of oppression and terrorized and economically exploited black communities under the guise of protecting white womanhood, hyper black criminality, and self-defense. It wouldn't have mattered if blacks could have snuffed out all the crime and violence within their communities; whites would have simply invented another excuse to oppress them.

This respectability mindset encouraged even staunch antiracist black activists to single out the poorest, least educated, and most socially vulnerable members of black communities for ridicule. The tenacity of this mindset is reflected in Bill Cosby's infamous 2004 NAACP keynote address where he essentially blames the black poor for perpetuating racist stereotypes and fueling white supremacy in the post–Civil Rights era and, more recently, in Charles Barkley's defense of white police brutality against blacks and vile description of Ferguson looters as "scum bags." As Ta-Nehisi Coates notes sardonically, "If aliens were to compare the socioeconomic realities of the black community with the history of their treatment in this country, they would not be mystified. Respectability politics is, at its root, the inability to look into the cold dark void of history. For if black people are—as I maintain—no part of the problem, if the problem truly is 100 percent explained by white supremacy, then we are presented with a set of unfortunate facts about our home."[28]

Accommodating the logic of white supremacist distraction then means perpetually chasing an unachievable goal of equality. Which is why appeals to respectability in the current era are as bankrupt as they were in the previous generations. As Coates rightly argues, property damage and looting "have been the most effective tools of social progress for white people in America."[29] The Boston Tea Party is one of the most revered revolutionary moments of our country's founding. More nefariously, whites have employed property damage and looting in a variety of ways "from enslavement to Jim Crow laws to lynching to redlining" to maintain their dominance over blacks and people of color. He further expounds: "'Property damage and looting'—perhaps more than nonviolence—has also been a significant tool in black 'social progress.' In 1851, when Shadrach Minkins was snatched off the streets of Boston under the authority of the Fugitive Slave Law, abolitionists 'stormed the courtroom' and 'overpowered the federal guards' to set Minkins free. That same year, when slaveholders came to Christiana, Pennsylvania to reclaim their property under the same law, they were not greeted with prayer and hymnals but with gunfire."[30]

Coates also astutely points out that the Student Nonviolent Coordinating Committee (SNCC) benefited greatly politically from the presence of Malcolm X during the Civil Rights Movement because they could leverage the threat of militancy he represented to whites to get them on board about nonviolent protest. As Coates writes, "Violence, lingering on the outside, often backed nonviolence during the Civil Rights Movement."[31] What should become clear at this point is that white expressions of protest in the form of looting and property damage is understood and evaluated through a radically different cultural lens than protests of the same sort by blacks. Keep in mind, Frederick Douglass was taking white liberals to task for a version of this racial double-standard thinking concerning slavery *over* a century ago. Which is to say that what we are witnessing today in the ways that the mainstream media is covering and characterizing black uprisings—and particularly the property damage that sometimes occurs as a consequence—is just the latest version of racial distraction. Which explains why, to invoke McKesson's phrasing, the mainstream media is more comfortable with debates about the problems of "broken windows" and the ruckus behavior of a small portion of black protesters than debates about the problems of "broken [black] spines" and the long and troubling legacy of white supremacist policing that ignites such uprisings.

Conclusion

Given that we no longer live in an overtly racially desegregated society, it is tempting for most whites to see our current state of existence as progress. But dominant ideologies, like plaque on our teeth, never ultimately go away. Stop caring for your teeth today and you are bound to get cavities in short order no matter how consistently you have taken care of your teeth in the past. We should not be surprised then that many hard-fought Civil Rights victories have been rolled back even *with* an antiracist black man in the White House for two terms; that whites' faith in the police has skyrocketed as a result of recent blue-on-black lethal interactions; that the net worth between blacks and whites is ever widening; and that a racial hatemonger and xenophobe like Donald Trump can galvanize the white masses and get elected to the highest office in the land following on the heels of the first black presidency. Indeed, as Michelle Alexander reminds us in *The New Jim Crow*, more African American adults "are under correctional control today—in prison or jail, on probation or parole—than were enslaved in 1850, a decade before the Civil War began."[32] Suffice it to say, this latest assault on black humanity in the form of white police brutality is, in fact, quite old—a continuation of a long-standing practice of harassing and terrorizing blacks into compliance.

While there are no easy solutions to centuries-old problems such as this, we can take heart in the show of support and solidarity against white supremacist policing in the United States on display worldwide. Even more promising is that the fiercest and most effective protests in the United States are being organized by young and gifted black folks. The youth are clearly awake. Those gatekeepers of black respectability would do well to take some political cues from King when it comes to engaging looting, violence, and the frustrations of young adults. Besides, to return to an early point by Coates, looting and violence have proven to be quite effective at times as a strategy for attaining justice. In fact, black hell-raising in response to Mike Brown's death is chiefly responsible for bringing the event into the national and international spotlight. So when so-called black leaders like President Obama and Al Sharpton focus attention on looting and militant reactions to white supremacist policing they bolster the white supremacist distraction discourse and undermine the legitimacy of black outrage. The fact that both men have lost significant credibility with many young activists as a result of this preoccupation with denouncing looting and violence responses is actually a good sign. It means that those young activists are hip on some conscious level to how white supremacist distraction works. Even though the odds of ending these brutal patterns of white supremacist policing are stacked against us at the moment, the show of resistance sends a powerful message to the world over that blacks will defend, respect, and celebrate our lives with the same intensity as our white peers defend, respect, and celebrate theirs. One thing is for damn certain: if we do not continue to fight to make black lives matter, no one else will.

FOUR

"Only Tired I Was, Was Tired of Giving In": Rosa Parks, Magical Negroes, and the Whitewashing of Black Struggle

The architects, visionaries, prime movers, and most of the on-the-ground labor-ers of the Civil Rights Movement were African American. Many white Americans stood beside them, and some even died beside them, but it was not their fight—and more important, it was not their idea.   MARTHA SOUTHGATE, "THE TRUTH ABOUT THE CIVIL RIGHTS ERA"

To protect [white] viewers, sometimes at profound damage to the historical re-cord, white heroes are featured and sometimes concocted for these [feel-good Civil Rights] movies, giving blacks a supporting role in their own struggle for lib-eration.   NELSON GEORGE, "BLACK AND WHITE STRUGGLE WITH A ROSY GLOW"

Until the lions have their own historians, tales of the hunt shall always glorify the hunters.   AFRICAN PROVERB

What did you learn in school today? These are typically the first words out of my mouth when I pick up my children, Elijah (fourteen) and Octavia (ten), from school. Though the obvious motivation behind the question is to moni-tor my children's academic development and engage, if not challenge, them intellectually to strive for excellence, I also want to monitor their cultural programming and set the record straight when need be about the plight of people of color and African Americans in particular. As public education in our society—now as always—pivots on nationalizing students out of the gate (the first thing that kindergarteners learn to memorize besides the alphabet is the "Pledge of Allegiance") and propagates American exceptionalism and whitewashed notions of history, literature, and culture, nary a day goes by that I'm not debunking half-truths or gross distortions about nonwhite realities that my children have been taught in the classroom. Suffice it to say, that I have ruffled more than a few feathers in my children's school and school district. Because I stress cultural literacy in my home and, indeed, encourage my children to exercise a healthy level of skepticism about their formal education, especially as it concerns representing racial realities, they have come to expect me to fill in and, in some cases, contest the cultural indoctrination that they receive in school. One of the most illuminating experiences on this front, for myself and my children, occurred when my son Elijah—nine years old at the time—came home one day during black history month bubbling over to share what he had learned about black history in class that day. Before I could even ask my customary question, he proffered a lesson that his class had been taught about Civil Rights icon Rosa Parks. "She desegregated a bus," my son said, stressing the word "desegregated" in what was clearly an attempt to impress his old man. "Before the Civil Rights Movement black people had to give up their bus seats to white people. But one day this old lady Rosa Parks was tired from a long day of work and decided she wasn't going to give her seat up to a white person. She was arrested and then motivated everybody to stop being unfair to African Americans. She also marched with Martin Luther King Jr."

Though his enthusiasm for black history was certainly encouraging, I was underwhelmed by the romanticized version of Parks and the Civil Rights Movement that he had been taught. "Did your teacher explain that Rosa Parks was not the first woman to be arrested for desegregating the buses in Birmingham? Did she tell you that Parks was only forty-two when she was arrested; that Parks and her husband were longtime Civil Rights activists; that she also believed in armed self-defense and expressed serious reservations about nonviolent protest? Did your teacher explain that Parks's protest was part of a larger civil rights strategy to desegregate the buses in Birmingham and bring racial equality to the city at large?"

My precocious and fair-minded child was indignant: "No, dad, she didn't tell us any of that! That's not right? Tell me the rest of the story, then," he pleaded earnestly. "I'll do you one better," I responded, reveling in the teaching moment. "I'll order a copy of Rosa Parks's autobiography today and let you read it for yourself." Though Elijah was less than thrilled that I was going to make him earn his knowledge rather than just supply him with it, he threw himself into reading the book when it arrived in the mail two days later. I was in the middle of preparing dinner when he galloped into the kitchen with book in hand and a look of outrage across his face. "Daddy, listen to this!" he said breathlessly. He was referencing an episode in the book when Parks was recounting what was running through her mind the moment she decided not to give up her seat on the bus and face arrest or worse. He began to read:

I thought back to the time when I used to sit up all night and didn't sleep, and my grandfather would have his gun right by the fireplace, or if he had his one-horse wagon going anywhere, he always had his gun in the back of the wagon. People always say I didn't give up my seat because I was tired, but that isn't true. I was not tired physically, or no more tired than I usually was at the end of a working day. I was not old, although some people have an image of me as being old then. I was forty-two. No, the only tired I was, was tired of giving in.[1]

My son's epiphany was beautiful. He was able to identify the clash between the whitewashed official narrative that is perpetuated in schools and the public domain and the actual truth of history as told by Rosa Parks. He also learned that Parks was acutely aware of the orchestrated misinformation about her activism. Equally as important, he was able to get a more nuanced understanding of Parks's racial politics, including her belief in armed self-defense. Indeed, my son honed in on Parks's repeated references to her gun-wielding grandfather who believed strongly in armed self-defense and how he was her primary source of inspiration and courage as she faced down white policemen and the looming threat of white terrorism during her protest. What perhaps shocked Elijah the most was Parks's deep respect for Malcolm X and his armed self-defense philosophy and, conversely, her deep ambivalence about King's near-fanatical investment in nonviolent protest. Raised to see armed self-defense in the face of white oppression as necessary and courageous, Parks had difficulty at times reconciling her notions of black self-determination with King's refusal to even defend himself when personally assaulted.[2] As her reflections on her grandfather clearly reveal, she was raised not only to stand up to whites but also to defend herself with lethal force if need be. Nonviolent resistance, then, was a strategy that Parks employed out of political expediency rather than ideological conviction. Armed self-defense was in her blood.

Magical-Negro Trope

Metonymically, the whitewashing of Parks's human complexity, personal history, and political radicalism reflects the tenacity and danger of what I refer to as the magical-negro trope. As noted in the Introduction, magical negroes function ideologically as sidekicks, good luck charms, spiritual forces, and the like whose raison d'être in white redemption narratives is to support/heal/ enlighten/inspire the white character(s) in crisis. As the whitewashing and recasting of black activists from slavery to the present day makes clear, this magical-negro trope is not limited politically to movies and novels. It operates on multiple real and symbolic levels to ensconce or subordinate black agency and self-determination to white concerns and desires. Indeed, the magical-negro trope turns black political radicalism into white fairy tales of racial inclusion and cooperation. As with all dominant ideologies, white supremacist ideology absorbs opposition. So, even though racial oppression, white supremacy, and capitalist patriarchy are the social, cultural, and political bedrocks of our country, the dominant narrative treats them as aberrations. Not surprisingly, redeeming whites are at the center of these narratives, making it appear that blacks are indebted to them for empowerment and self-determination. For example, these narratives treat slavery as an unfortunate but ultimately positive phenomenon for enslaved Africans in America as it transitioned them from the primitivism of the African jungle to the modernization of (white) Western Civilization; they grossly misrepresent Abraham Lincoln as an antislavery martyr; and routinely conflate elite whites across time who held at best moderately progressive racial agendas (and in many instances did very little substantively for black people) with serious antiracist change agents. Again, as the slave master schoolteacher reminds the slave Sixo in Toni Morrison's *Beloved*, "definitions belong to the definers not the defined."[3]

In this chapter I will first contextualize the origins of the magical-negro trope and engage critically the racial logics and political utility that allow it to hide in plain sight. Of critical importance is establishing that the magical-negro trope is not an inexplicable phenomenon. Indeed, whites invented and deployed this trope to empower themselves to misrepresent consciously and unconsciously African Americans' plight, including denying the devastating consequences that white capitalist patriarchy and centuries of state-sanctioned racial terrorism have wreaked on black consciousness and self-determination. The chapter concludes by engaging the productive and potentially revolutionary ways that blacks have responded over time to this trope and the gross distortions of African Americans' plight in this country that the trope was designed to perpetuate. What will become clear is that blacks are not only acutely aware of this trope but are actively working to expose and dismantle it across multiple mediums.

The trope of the magical negro grows directly out of the white supremacist myth of the faithful slave. As Micki McElya explains, the myth of the faithful slave functioned ideologically and politically to cover over the reality of white atrocities against captive and enslaved Africans:

Accounts of enslaved peoples' fidelity constituted the ultimate expression of southern paternalism, which held that the relationship of the masters to the slave was removed from market forces and economic exigency and functioned more like a familial relationship between father and child based on a set of mutual obligations and responsibilities as well as affection. The faithful slave narrative . . . went one step further to argue that enslaved people appeared faithful and caring not because they had to be or were violently compelled to be, but because their fidelity was heartfelt and indicative of their love for and dependence on their owners. At their core, stories of faithful slaves were expressions of the value, honor, and identity of whites. They had little if anything to do with the actual perceptions and attitudes of the enslaved.[4]

McElya offers key insights here into willful white blindness and, more specifically, why tropes of faithful slaves/magical negroes continue to have cultural currency today. Whites across class lines—then and now—have a major ideological stake in viewing their dominance in society—which came about in large part because of military might, racial terrorism, and economic coercion—as the stuff of meritocracy and rugged individualism. To emerge as the "good guys" in the narrative of American history, then, they must contend with the reality of slavery, imperialist dominance over indigenous populations, and the like. Redemptive narratives of white goodwill and faithful slaves function ideologically in the present day to discredit counterhegemonic narratives—such as slave narratives, antiracist novels, blogs, and even politically inflected rap music—and encourages whites to feel good about their position of socioeconomic dominance. The magical-negro trope is an extension of this whitewashing ideological enterprise.

Because what we experience as real is inextricably tethered to what we have been conditioned and policed to experience as real, it is often an uphill battle to get even oppressed people to see how white suprema-cist apparatuses like the magical-negro trope have altered their percep-tions of self-determination, personal accountability, meritocracy, institu-tional racism, and reality itself. W. E. B. Du Bois explained this ideological phenomenon as an outgrowth of what he famously called "double con-sciousness"—a phenomenon of racial conditioning whereby blacks see their actions and behaviors and that of their black peers through the "eyes" of whites who look upon them with "amused contempt and pity." What Du Bois brings to light (albeit in decidedly male-centric ways)[5] is that ideological struggle for blacks in a radically raced society is to "rec-oncile" the cultural contradiction that is their status as black Americans. To be an American is by default to be white and invested in white su-premacy and to be black is by default to be an othered American and deemed culturally inferior. For Du Bois the challenge for African Ameri-cans is how to be an American citizen without having to embrace white supremacy or, by extension, view one's African ancestry as a malady or mark of shame:

The history of the American Negro is the history of this strife—this longing to attain self-conscious manhood, to merge his double self into a better and truer self. In this merging he wishes neither of the older selves to be lost. He does not wish to Africanize America, for America has too much to teach the world and Africa. He wouldn't bleach his Negro blood in a flood of white Americanism, for he knows that Negro blood has a message for the world. He simply wishes to make it possible for a man to be both a Negro and an American without being cursed and spit upon by his fellows, without having the doors of opportunity closed roughly in his face.[6]

Du Bois treats this dilemma of double consciousness as a conundrum: how does the African American embrace the best of both worlds, being an American and a person of African descent. The core problem that goes unspoken here is that white supremacist ideology depends on this perpetual othering of blacks and other communities of color. The main-tenance of the status quo of white dominance is indeed tied to keeping blacks in this perpetual and ultimately unachievable pursuit of white validation or what I referred to in chapter 3 as "racial distraction." Which explains why, say, mainstream media discussions of the unconscionable killing of Trayvon Martin by self-deputized white supremacist George Zimmerman often collapsed into absurd debates about black men's ur-ban dress and thug cultural mindset being the ultimate culprit instead of institutionalized white supremacy and the pathologizing of young urban black men and boys. In other words, Trayvon Martin and urban black men were put on trial and ultimately held responsible—literally and figuratively—for why white fear of black violence justified the use of lethal force even in cases like the murder of Martin where armed whites initiate confrontations with unarmed and law-abiding blacks. State-sanctioned murdering of black men and boys is compounded by the fact that a cadre of black respectability gatekeepers and white supremacist apologists, including Charles Barkley, Don Lemon, Ben Carson, and Stephen A. Smith, defended the twisted thesis of white fear and pathological black urban men and boys. Notably, if not predictably, the mainstream media rarely interviews blacks who have actual expertise on these matters. (Cornel West is perhaps one of the few notable exceptions and his seemingly personal beef with President Obama and his supporters has made him somewhat of a pariah in black spaces when it comes to this issue.) That black twitter has emerged in recent times as a more reliable source of news and critical social discussions about race, racism, and white supremacy for African Americans is very telling in this regard.

Pedagogically speaking, I often explain this phenomenon of twisted racial logic to my mostly white students in nonracial terms as a way to help them wrap their minds around how white supremacist ideology and the magical-negro trope operate. I also do so because white fragility often frustrates even the most earnest white students' ability to understand black oppression and own their relationship to it. Indeed, my white students tend to respond emotionally to such informed critiques of whiteness and white privilege in a defensive, if not hostile, manner. I ask them how they would feel if one of their women peers were to show up to class topless. Most confess they would feel extremely uncomfortable, if not outright scandalized by the spectacle. I then explain to them that the feelings of shame, outrage, and embarrassment that such an act would provoke is a product of learned behavior—behavior that is so vigorously policed that we experience it as natural. I then remind them that there are still cultures that do not automatically draw a link between breasts, eroticism, and primitivism as many (white) Westernized societies do; that puritanical Western societies have historically introduced and imposed these cultural notions onto tribes and countries—particularly in the Southern Hemisphere—that have come under their military rule and social dominance. My larger point is simply this: we cannot rely uncritically on the "genuineness" of our experiences to make sense of reality. This is the tricky magic, if you will, of ideology: to make socially manufactured ideas appear commonsensical and normative. What woman in her right mind would deign to go topless in public? We have terms in our cultural lexicon for such women and ain't none of them nice.

The discourse of race—even for those who are negatively impacted by it—is equally slippery, if profoundly more insidious. The magical-negro trope remains ideologically vibrant today for one simple reason—white supremacy, though no longer acceptable to publicly advocate, continues to have significant cultural capital, especially as it concerns white self-esteem and agency. In other words, the dominant and policed notion that there is something inherently superior about whiteness depends parasitically on othering blackness. A black colleague of mine put it best when he quipped in a discussion with a white student about race relations that "I'm black *only* because you insist on being white."[7] Morrison's theory of "American Africanisms" spells out this parasitical relationship in addition to explaining why it is so difficult for even informed and critical-thinking black folks to identify and resist it. In particular, she uses the theory to expose the racial othering phenomenon wherein white-generated and contradictory notions of captive Africans as primitive, violent, docile, ultrareligious, pathological, subservient, promiscuous, and childlike operate to authenticate white superiority and give cultural capital to dominant notions of freedom, masculinity, womanhood, self-determination, justice, and inalienable rights. Morrison avers that the "conveniently bound and violently silenced black bodies" were the mediums by and through which artists and white society at large sorted out and grappled with the inherent contradictions of their new experimental society which was premised on ideals of democracy and self-determination that were radically out of sync with socioeconomic realities on the ground, including slavery and profound class disparities among whites. Focusing on the highly coveted and ballyhooed concept of American freedom, she notes, "Nothing highlighted freedom—if it did not in fact create it—like slavery."[8] She further expounds, "Black slavery enriched the country's creative possibilities. For in that construction of blackness *and* enslavement could be found not only the not-free but also, with the dramatic polarity created by skin color, the projection of the not-me. The result was a playground for the imagination. What rose up out of collective needs to allay internal fears and to rationalize external exploitation was American Africanism—a fabricated brew of darkness, otherness, alarm, and desire that is uniquely American."[9]

If anything, the trope of the magical negro grows directly out of this ideological impulse to displace white anxieties and fears about a range of entities—including the false social realities that are American exceptionalism, democracy, and freedom—onto blackness. Parks and other white-washed historical figures like Harriet Tubman, Frederick Douglass, and Martin Luther King Jr. are more palatable ideologically to the dominant culture, then, because the magical-negro trope uncouples their complex humanities as self-actualized, revolutionary, fearless and transformative agents from the social, political and cultural significance of their human rights activism. I am reminded of a ten-year-old African American honors student Malik (not his real name) whom I was mentoring in 2001 as a graduate student in Madison, Wisconsin. Malik's knowledge of black history was so skewed that he once told me that Martin Luther King Jr. freed the slaves through the Underground Railroad. Mind you, Malik was a high-performing student. His ignorance reflected the inadequacy of his education about black American history, not a lack of intelligence. Considering the whitewashed versions of black history children receive during their formal schooling, it should come as no surprise that even a high-performing student like Malik could confuse Martin Luther King Jr. with Harriet Tubman. The tenacity of the magical-negro trope combined with the decidedly low expectation of critical engagement from school systems mean that what little children do learn about black history reinforces the status quo of postracialism in the twenty-first century rather than challenges it.

It is also important to note that the magical-negro trope exists, in part, to neutralize white violence that cannot so easily be covered. Take the gruesome murder of fourteen-year-old Emmett Till in 1955, for example, which occurred just down the road from Birmingham, Alabama, in Money, Mississippi, and just three months before Parks's historic protest. Emmett Till was viciously murdered when he allegedly deigned to interact with a white woman in a perceived flirtatious way. Till's white murderers, Roy Bryant and his brother-in-law J. W. Milam, were not only acquitted of all wrongdoing by an all-white jury but went on to become police officers. Emmett Till's accuser, Carolyn Bryant Donham, admitted in 2016 that she lied about her encounter with Till and regretted her role in his murder. Protected from prosecution because of double jeopardy, Bryant and Milam later confessed to the murder in *Look* magazine for a purported fee of $4,000. That's nearly $35,500 today when adjusted for inflation. The cold reality is that most Americans under the age of forty have probably never heard of Emmett Till. If Parks, King, Tubman, and Douglass's historical realities are culturally re-scripted to accommodate the narrative of colorblind democracy, American exceptionalism, racial inclusiveness, and the like, Emmett Till's historical reality is erased altogether. Though I doubt we have access to information about how many school districts across the country teach about Till, I would venture to say very few. I doubt even that most teachers (especially white ones) even know the history of Till unless they majored in African American/Africana studies in college. Of course, even if a teacher was knowledgeable about Till's gruesome murder and its historical significance to the Civil Rights Movement, he or she would not necessarily have the green light to teach it. As we have witnessed of late with the renewed and growing national attention to the criminalization of African American communities and militarization of the police force, it is increasingly more difficult to engage in critical discussions about race and race matters in public school settings. States like Arizona and Texas have in fact made significant political moves to whitewash the history of American slavery. In 2010 Arizona succeeded, in fact, in passing a bill that penalizes any school district that teaches ethnic studies. Governor Jan Brewer, who signed the bill, argued that ethnic studies courses teach students "to resent or hate other races."[10] Further, in 2016 state senators David Murphy and Steve Nass, chair and vice chair of the Committee on Universities and Technical Colleges, attacked an assistant professor in African Studies at the University of Wisconsin-Madison, Damon Sajnani, for his course entitled "The Problems of Whiteness." Though whiteness studies is a long-established field of inquiry and Sajnani is highly qualified to teach it, having received his doctorate in African American studies and sociology from Northwestern University, Murphy (who consequently doesn't even have a bachelor's degree) and Nass represented the course as antiwhite and insinuated that Sajnani was racist for teaching it. When UW-Madison officials defended the course and the academic freedom of university professors, Murphy and Nass launched a veritable smear campaign, dredging up controversial tweets Sajnani made about the Black Lives Matter movement and whiteness, and began calling for the professor to be fired. They also floated the idea that the state legislature should consider withholding funding to the university if it didn't comply with their requests.[11] While Sajnani and the whiteness course seem safe for now (Governor Scott Walker, who effectively destroyed tenure at UW-Madison and almost single-handedly eroded its academic reputation and ranking, is not co-signing the move though he has referred to the class as "goofy" and "unusual"),[12] a clear and dangerous message about academic freedom and white supremacy has been communicated.

What is really at stake in these political attacks and insidious maneuvers is the preservation of white supremacist ideology and, specifically, raced notions of American exceptionalism, inclusiveness, and white redemption. The urgency of this preservation is compounded by the white-anxiety-producing browning of America, which is highly evident in states like Arizona, California, North Carolina, Georgia, and Wisconsin. The election of Donald Trump to the presidency—a rich elite white man who embodies this white supremacist thinking and revels in attacking vulnerable groups—means that we can expect such attacks to become more frequent and intense in the coming years, if not also gain political and cultural legitimacy.

The political utility of the magical-negro trope vis-à-vis such horrific accounts of historical white terrorism was brought radically into focus during a conversation in 2004 with a white male colleague in my department who also had small children. Though my colleague did not have a problem letting his children watch violent television programs or play violent video games, he waxed indignant when I informed him that I was teaching my children—who were then five and nine—about Emmett Till and the bloody history of blacks' human rights struggle in this country. To his way of thinking, exposing his children to the harsh racial realities of our countries past and present threatened to rob them of their innocence. This was an individual—mind you—who had written a scholarly book on race, African American identity, and nature. What he was essentially protecting his children from was learning about the source of their white privilege. He had the social and cultural luxury of "shielding" his children from the realities of racial inequality because the stakes for his children's health and well-being were low to nonexistent.

As whiteness and indeed white supremacy are rendered normative in our society, "shielding" one's white child from the realities of racial inequality is by default perpetuating the idea of whiteness and white supremacy as normative. There is no racial middle ground. White supremacist ideology will not allow for it. Namely, because white supremacist ideology is parasitically dependent on the idea of a fixed black inferior. I cannot afford to let my children invest in status quo thinking about self-determination, social justice, knowledge, intellect, and even fairy tales and Christian mythology, because such thinking conveys the detrimental message that African Americans are inherently corrupt, amoral, anti-intellectual and pathological. Shrouding my children from the social, cultural, and material realities of race and racism in the United States is a "luxury" as an African American parent that I can ill afford. Indeed, I would go so far as to say that doing so borders on irresponsible parenting. Consider the tragic case of twelve-year-old Tamir Rice. Rice was shot and killed in a park in Cleveland playing with a toy gun. Though the white policeman who murdered this child, Timothy A. Loehmann, did not take as much as three seconds to assess the situation before opening fire (a video recording of the scene confirming as much), the stance by the Cleveland police department is chillingly consistent with other such cases—they are standing by the officer and hoisting the blame on the murdered victim. For those who see dash and body cameras in police cars as a viable way to curb racist policing, Rice's killing, like Eric Garner's, *was* recorded. Indeed, as we discussed in chapter 3, white support for policemen has risen substantially since these highly publicized cases of white-on-black lethal interactions between police officers and civilians. Because my white colleague's children will likely never be in a situation in which they will treated with such aggressive police violence and social dismissal—since, in fact, the police and judicial system are ostensibly designed to privilege whiteness—he need not caution his children against, well, being children and doing the things that many children do, like playing with toy guns, bows and arrows, or swords.

Lovable Racists and History as Propaganda

In *The Fire Next Time* James Baldwin explains how white supremacist ideology hijacks the historical narrative of black social struggle, genius, and political success. Referring to the 1954 Supreme Court decision to outlaw segregation in the schools, he avers that whites "congratulate themselves" on the decision despite the "mountain of evidence" demonstrating that a host of factors, including black agitation nationally, "the competition of the Cold War," and the widespread liberation movements across Africa, forced their hands. He rightly argues that had the Supreme Court decision been a "matter of love or justice" it would "surely have occurred sooner" and had it not been for these major global factors, "it might very well not have occurred yet." He concludes, "The sloppy and fatuous nature of American good will can never be relied upon to deal with hard problems. These have been dealt with, when they have been dealt with at all, out of necessity—and in political terms, anyway, necessity means concessions made in order to stay on top."[13] What Baldwin brings starkly into focus is the propensity for white supremacist power to co-opt black political agency and, indeed, any challenge to white socioeconomic dominance, to reflect white political, social, and economic interests. Concessions made within the white supremacist calculus are not ultimately about conceding power but rather negotiating resistance in ways that pacifies the oppressed even as it reinscribes the goals and values of the oppressors.

Baldwin's insights here bring to mind some advice my late mentor Nellie McKay humorously bestowed upon me when I was first on the job market as a college professor in 2002. She quipped that I should view the black cultural center buildings on campus as a litmus test for the racial climate; the more structurally impressive the black cultural center the more likely there were significant racial problems on the campus. The cultural joke, as it were, was that many colleges and universities used black cultural center buildings as bartering chips to pacify black social unrest and political agitation. Read through this cultural lens, a high-priced, ornately constructed cultural center may indicate how much the institution thought it needed to "invest" to quell black agitation/social unrest rather than how much it was actually committed to diversity and inclusiveness. Consequently, the University of Tennessee-Knoxville, where I landed my first academic job, has one of the most impressive black cultural studies buildings in the country. Shortly after taking the job, I learned that the UT higher education system had been successfully sued for its discriminating practices in hiring and retaining black faculty and admitting students and was operating under a five-year multimillion dollar "Geier consent decree," named in honor of black civil rights pioneer Dr. Rita Geier, who initiated the lawsuit. In 2002, when I started at the university, the consent decree against the UT system had been in effect for only a year. My suspicion is that the bright and shiny new black cultural center the English department made sure I toured when I came to campus for my interview was built with Geier consent decree funding. In a word, it was a racial concession borne of black social and political protest, as was probably the aggressive recruitment of a black African Americanist scholar, like myself, as well. Suffice it to say, Nellie McKay was a very wise woman.

To return to Baldwin's argument, the political reality is that whites could not control the fact that certain black activists and groups were elevated to hero status among blacks but what they could and did control were the social and political terms upon which that heroism was recognized and legitimated. For instance, when the Civil Rights Movement is taught at the secondary level, students are routinely steered away from focusing on or engaging critically with white supremacist ideology and its gruesome political, social, economic, and cultural outcomes for blacks and people of color in general. To wit, most students have probably never heard of COINTELPRO and the havoc that J. Edgar Hoover, the head of the FBI, wreaked on civil rights organizations in the 1950s and beyond. This havoc included illegally spying on, infiltrating, and dismantling civil rights organizations that the FBI and Hoover in particular deemed subversive like SCLC, NAACP, CORE, and SNCC. Most egregiously, the Hoover-led FBI attempted to tarnish the reputation of the Civil Rights and Black Power movements' most visible leaders like Martin Luther King Jr., Huey Newton, Malcolm X, and Rosa Parks, to name but a few. Despite the fact that this and other subversive government-led programs have now come to light, the conventional history of the Civil Rights

Movement—that is, the history that is taught to the majority of children in the United States—tends not to engage with this unflattering aspect of our racial past. Thus even though the (white) state apparatuses of power could not dismantle the Civil Rights Movement, they managed over time to control the terms upon which we commemorate and teach it. Indeed, these state apparatuses of power have made concessions even out of hard-fought social changes, like the establishment of black history month, making Martin Luther King Jr.'s birthday a federal holiday, and the erection of monuments in Washington DC in honor of Martin Luther King Jr. and Rosa Parks. It bears repeating that it took the blood, sweat, and tears on behalf of many African Americans activists, citizens, and politicians and, in some cases, their white allies to turn the aforementioned holidays, monuments, and commemorations into realities. These hard-fought accomplishments are ultimately concessions in a Baldwinian sense because state apparatuses of power have hijacked and re-scripted their historical import. As Rev. Joseph Lowery averred at Coretta Scott King's funeral, "Dead men make such convenient heroes. They cannot rise up to challenge the images we mold and fashion for them."[14] Alas, Lowery's observations do not go far enough. Parks was very much alive and well when her radical act of civil disobedience was being hijacked and re-scripted to accommodate notions of American exceptionalism and white redemption by state apparatuses of white power. Ostensibly written to set the record straight about her now iconic act of civil disobedience, Parks's autobiography, *Rosa Parks: My Story* (1992), was ultimately ineffective in discrediting the established whitewashed versions. The tenacity of the magical-negro trope cannot be overstated.

Even though he was concerned more generally with exposing and countering how white Western literature operated as antiblack propaganda, W. E. B. Du Bois's iconic 1926 speech "Criteria for Negro Art" provides useful insights into why it is so crucial—then as now—to attack the magical-negro trope. In his speech Du Bois implores young black artists to create propagandistic art that conveys blacks in the most redeeming light possible. After declaring that all art is propaganda, he asserts, "I stand in utter shamelessness and say that whatever art I have for writing has been used always for propaganda for gaining the right of black folk to love and enjoy. I do not care a damn for any art that is not used for propaganda. But I do care when propaganda is confined to one side while the other is stripped and silent."[15]

At first blush, Du Bois's art-as-propaganda rallying cry seems constraining to black artistic expression. But Du Bois is calling attention to the extricable link between art and ideologies of power and pointing out the ways in which what passes as high art is determined by the white gaze. Because white humanity is rendered normative within white supremacist ideology, the white artist has the freedom to create art without cultural limits. In contrast, black humanity is pathologized and rendered deviant within white supremacist ideology, meaning that only certain aspects of black humanity—namely those that cast blacks in an inferior posture vis-à-vis whites—register as legitimate and receive any recognition by mainstream publishing outlets.

Magical-negro characters such as Harriet Beecher Stowe's Uncle Tom in *Uncle Tom's Cabin* and nigger Jim in Mark Twain's *Huckleberry Finn* were no doubt the kinds of whitewashed black "redeeming" characters in white fiction that Du Bois was referencing as propaganda and directing his venom. Even if we grant that Du Bois was, if not an elitist, certainly a gatekeeper of black respectability, his point is difficult to refute. The genius of many twentieth-century black artists, including Zora Neale Hurston, Langston Hughes, and James Baldwin, was not recognized as such in their day because the value of their writing was often determined by white critics, including those with liberal political leanings and white-centric world views. (Many of these artists were also, consequently, dependent as artists on the financial largesse of wealthy white donors, most notably Charlotte Osgood Mason, who often operated in a paternalistic manner and referred to black art endearingly as "primitive.") In this speech, Du Bois tells the story of how a young black artist's short story about the travails of a black middle-class family was initially rejected by a mainstream white literary magazine editor who found the story contrived. However, when the author resubmitted a version of the same story (under an assumed name), making all the characters white and changing the setting to a white locale, then the same white editor not only enthusiastically accepted it, he encouraged the author to submit more of his work to the magazine. Du Bois argues that the mechanism of evaluation is radically raced and designed to police white superiority and black inferiority. He makes a compelling case to the young black artists in the room that blacks have to become less dependent on white judgment and establish their own standards of excellence:

The ultimate judge has got to be you and you have got to build yourselves up into that wide judgment, that catholicity of temper which is going to enable the artist to have his widest chance for freedom. . . . As it is now we are handing everything over to a white jury. If a colored man wants to publish a book, he has got to get a white publisher and a white newspaper to say it is great; and then you and I say so. We must come to the place where the work of art when it appears is reviewed and acclaimed

by our own free and unfettered judgment. And we are going to have a real and valuable and eternal judgment only as we make ourselves free of mind, proud of body and
just of soul to all men.[16]

Achieving black artistic freedom is thus paradoxical for Du Bois. Black
artists cannot get to the point to which they can enjoy the liberty to create art on their own terms without creating a cultural medium to affirm
the value and richness of their artistic expressions. Though again we can
certainly take issue with what constituted great art for Du Bois (Zora Neale
Hurston's *Their Eyes Were Watching God* would likely not have qualified
in his eyes because of her use of black dialect and "racy" themes), his
analysis of how white supremacist ideology determines artistic merit
and value and the need for alternative critical model of evaluation is on
point. This critique can easily be applied to our cultural environment
today. The composition of the Academy Awards voting members is a
radical case in point. According to the *L.A. Times*, as of 2012 more than
94 percent of the 5,765 voting members of the Academy Awards are
white; only 2 percent are black and 2 percent Latino. Moreover, the me-
dian age of voters is sixty-two, meaning that the majority of these white
voters grew up during the height of the Jim Crow era.[17] Considering
that blacks have received only 31 out the 2,809 Oscar/Academy awards
given since the Academy Awards show began in 1957 and Ava DuVernay
(whose direction of the Martin Luther King Jr. biopic *Selma* in 2015 was
superb) was just conspicuously passed over in the category of best director (which has never been awarded to a black woman), Du Bois's arguments about black art, propaganda, and artistic freedom seem almost
prescient.

While it is certainly frightening to consider how much has not changed
ideologically since Du Bois gave his speech nearly a century ago, I want
to end this chapter by highlighting the possibilities for social transforma-
tion via educating and empowering our youth. Earlier in the chapter I had
referenced my son's rude awakening regarding Rosa Parks and her radical
act of protest. Well, the story did not end with his simply gaining knowledge about Parks and becoming aware of the limits of his formal education, especially when it comes to racial matters. Elijah, like many ten-
year-olds, was understandably disturbed by learning of his white teacher's
misrepresentation of Parks. You see, Elijah really liked his teacher and,
frankly, so did I. She held him to a higher standard, always pushed him
to excel, and was at the same time incredibly supportive and encouraging. My initial impulse was to intervene and alert the teacher about the
problems of her pedagogy but Elijah had a different and, as it turned out,

much more effective strategy. He decided to use an upcoming public-speaking assignment in his class as an opportunity to debunk historical myths about Parks. The assignment required each student to deliver an eight-minute speech to the class. The day after Elijah delivered his speech his teacher did a special segment on Rosa Parks, which included acknowledging her misrepresentations and delving even deeper into Parks's history. During her new history lesson she also gave Elijah credit for helping her to see the limits of her knowledge about Parks. Elijah had not only schooled his teacher but demonstrated that given the adequate critical tools to think through these issues he could develop strategies independent of his father's to negotiate white supremacist ideology.

If we have any hope of exploding the magical-negro trope and attendant white supremacist thinking in the twenty-first century, we have to equip our children with the necessary critical tools to empower themselves and others. If not us then who? If not now, then when? Our children are literally being murdered in the streets in the name of law and order and the dominant white response nationally has been *increased* support and confidence in our policing and judicial systems. Moreover, the white majority also just elected a white man in Donald Trump who unapologetically championed the policing practice of "Stop and Frisk" which the US District Courts ruled unconstitutional in 2013 because it was a form of racial profiling. The jury, as the colloquium goes, is in: whites as a collective have no intention of acknowledging their historic culpability in our subordination. And as we have witnessed firsthand, when it comes to addressing the plight of black Americans a black status quo president like Obama (who depended and depends on a significant portion of this white population for financial, social, and political support) is of little consequence beyond cementing whitewashed notions of American exceptionalism and self-determination. To invoke June Jordan's "Poem for South African Women" (that, ironically enough, President Obama was fond of quoting on his two successful presidential campaigns), "we are the ones we have been waiting for."[18]

If progress is to be made on these many racial fronts, we have to be the ones to make it. What this means beyond continuing the fight for social justice and racial equality in all facets of our society is that we have to remain vigilant and steadfast in pushing against the dominant society's misrepresentation of our history of struggle. Indeed, if we allow the dominant white supremacist institutions of power to continue to revise and define our history, they will continue to have the upper hand culturally, socially, and politically in defining our present and future. Rosa Parks understood this dynamic all too well and battled against the odds to set the record straight about her protest. While the whitewashed version of her monumental achievements still dominates in our public discourse, Parks left behind a slew of testimonials, including her autobiography, to deromanticize it. In other words, she refused to be silenced or defined by those who had much to gain from whitewashing her civil rights activism. We would do well to follow her lead.

FIVE

Santa Claus Is White and Jesus Is Too: Era(c)ing White Myths for the Health and Well-Being of Our Children

Yonder they do not love your flesh. They despise it. They don't love your eyes; they'd just as soon pick em out. No more do they love the skin on your back. . . . *You* got to love it, *you*! TONI MORRISON, *BELOVED*

I will never forget this tragic-comic moment in mid-December 2005. It occurred on a Saturday around 3 o'clock. I was sitting at my computer desk working feverishly to meet a publishing deadline. My former marriage partner was at the park with our three-year-old "crunk" son, Elijah. Indeed, she had graciously agreed to take him to the park for the afternoon, providing me with the rare opportunity to write on the weekend. When I heard the mechanical hum of the automatic garage door opening, I knew that my precious writing time was up. As I was pressing to wrap up the section on which I was working—hoping against hope that the mother of my children could entertain my precocious, high-energy three-year-old son Elijah for a few minutes more—I heard his little footsteps bounding up our staircase. When he darted in our home office and jumped on my lap—effectively ending my writing session—he looked up at me with a devilish grin and said, "Guess what happened at the park today?" "What?" I returned, glad to see his bright, bubbling face but also bemoaning internally that I had to cut my writing time short. "Somebody tried to tell me that Santa Claus was real." "Somebody did what?" I said, my interest suddenly piqued. "What are you doing up here," he said, shifting subjects midstream as three-year-olds are apt to do. "Writing," I said, "But, what happened at the park?" "Oh, yes. Some white woman asked me what Santa Claus was going to bring me for Christmas. I told her that I don't believe in that stuff. My parents buy my toys. Can I have a cookie?"

Before I could finish interviewing my son, his mother poked her head into the office and said with a slight edge to her voice, "We need to talk." After we gave our son a snack—the lobbied-for cookie with milk—and put him down for his nap, I was able to get the rest of the story. Turns out that the "someone" with whom my son spoke was actually an elderly white couple, strolling in the park with their infant grandchild. Socialite that he is, my son asked if he could see and touch the baby. After consenting to let him do so, the couple asked the aforementioned question about what my son expected to get from Santa. Elijah returned their "well-intended" query with a smirk. Looking from them to his mother and back again, he bellowed, "I don't believe in Santa Claus. My daddy says that a white man doesn't buy my presents. That him and momma do. You didn't know that?" The white couple gasped collectively and then shot the mother of my children a disapproving glance. After an awkward silence, the white couple replied that they hoped that my son's Christmas would be a good one whoever brought his presents and then they moved hurriedly along.

Though the decision to explode the Santa Claus myth for our son had been made jointly, albeit at my vehement urging, this was the first time that our "racial experiment" had been put to the test. And—perhaps despite herself—the mother of my children was feeling a bit embarrassed by the whole ordeal, if still supporting of our decision to disabuse our son of the myth. After having what amounted to a strategy/therapy session—in which we discussed the stress of progressive racial parenting and strategized ways to teach our son how to balance out his scrutiny with tactfulness—we sat down to coffee, and managed to find the humor in the absurdity of the event.

When I share this anecdote with my mostly white, Christian-identified students in the historically white university in which I teach, most are genuinely confused, if also rendered a bit uncomfortable by our racial empowerment parenting strategy. As one student so candidly put it, "Isn't believing in Santa Claus a good thing. The myth encourages children to be good. What does it have to do with race?" To be sure, the very framing of the question is politically loaded and racially skewed, as it assumes a priori that by fortifying my children against white myths I am *provoking* racial conflict rather than merely *reacting to* how our race-obsessed culture, at once, normalizes whiteness and pathologizes blackness. (Not to mention the Western Empire–steeped assumption that Christianity and its attendant myths are universal.) My response to this, and similarly couched questions, is Socratic. Which is to say, I answer their query with a query, placing the onus back on them to consider the context and subtext of their query. More specifically, I ask them what would happen if the (white) mall in the upper-class section of town used a black Santa Claus instead of a white one during promotional Christmas events. (This actually happened in 2016 at the Mall of America in Minnesota and the virulent racist backlash on social media and in the public domain made headlines.) Or, similarly, what would happen in their white churches if the Eurocentric versions of Jesus—those painted by Leonardo da Vinci, Fra Angelico, and Michelangelo—were replaced by a more historically plausible portrait of a brown man with Middle Eastern or Afrocentric features. The room usually goes quiet at this point, though recently a rather outspoken white student chimed in with a humorous twinge of irony that if I tried to replace white Jesus in his church I probably wouldn't make it out alive.

Typically at this juncture in the class discussion I open up about my own experiences as a child growing up in the Bible Belt corridor of rural North Carolina in the 1970s and 1980s to further underscore the deleterious and lasting effects of these seemingly benign white formulations on "raced" populations. The personal narrative I share with them—and will offer to contextualize my argument here—goes as follows: I grew up in a de facto segregated small town of Troutman, North Carolina, where blacks and whites literally lived on opposite sides of the railroad tracks that snaked through the middle of town. Whereas whites could and did—in small numbers—live on the black side of town, blacks could not—at least not safely—live on the white side of town. Indeed, the first Ku Klux Klan march I witnessed at the tender age of eight—a spectacle of hate the likes of which I cannot adequately capture in words—was organized in direct response to a black family "from up North" that bought a house on the "white" side of the tracks. No doubt traumatized by this organized force of racial intimidation, the black family packed their bags and moved, not just out of the house, but completely out of the South.

Intensifying the emotional pain of such experiences was the fact that I didn't have an interpretive critical model through which to process

111

these devastating emotional experiences. Isolated as I was culturally, racially, and intellectually (I literally didn't know that black people wrote books until I went to college in 1990), I was forced to rely on imposed racial discourses to frame my understanding of US society writ large. This is not to say that my parents and the black communities of which I was a part did not fight back. Because they surely did. The problem was that I—and they—had been inundated with racial imagines from virtually every facet of society that depicted whiteness as the literal and figurative embodiment of goodness, intelligence, fairness, wealth, and the like. It seemed self-evident at the time, then, that Jesus, the tooth fairy, all superheroes, and Santa Claus were white. So, on the one hand, whites were the proverbial "good guys," setting the standards—moral, cultural, political, and economical—upon which black folks were expected to aspire. And, on the other hand, they constituted the group that looked down on our community, who frequently called me "nigger" in the streets and at school, who marched in white sheets down Main Street proclaiming white supremacy, and whose presence largely dictated how we moved through our social spaces.

Sorting out these mixed racial messages—coupled, of course, with being inundated with portraits of black folks as immoral, lazy, parasitical, anti-intellectual, and oversexed—was a daunting task, given that my lived experience as a target of racism clashed sharply with my received images of white moral, intellectual, economic, and political superiority. Indeed, to this day—even though intellectually I know better[1]—when someone invokes the Judeo-Christian "god-figure" Jesus, the Leonardo da Vinci, Fra Angelico, and Michelangelo versions of "white Jesus" come automatically to mind. Understanding and disrupting this mind-game of race rendered through internalized white supremacy is in many regards a *more* pressing issue for black Americans than even the material consequences of structural inequality and un/conscious racial bias.

What about the Children?

It bears repeating that extant white superiority/black inferiority ideologies that encourage dominant and subordinate groups to see racial injustice and the like as organic or normative are equally as pressing a crisis as the actual material consequences of extant racial and structural inequalities. Indeed, because being white is still synonymous culturally with being "normal," the cultural programming of our children vis-à-vis whitewashed superheroes, myths, and religious figures typically flies under the radar of concern. It is arguably, then, more difficult in some ways for my children and black children in their age group generally to critically engage such cultural programming. Even though, like my generation, they are being taught to embrace these whitewashed superheroes, myths, and religious icons, they are also being taught they live in a postracial society and that the election of a black president and other such events are an irrefutable proof of this fact. And, to be clear, getting blacks to engage these issues is almost as daunting a task as getting white folks to do so. I liken it to educating the public about the dangers of sugar overconsumption. Big food corporations and fast food restaurant chains that stand to gain from our sugar addiction inundate us with misinformation and feel-good messages that obscure the real and pressing dangers, including obesity, high blood pressure, diabetes, heart attack, stroke, and the like. (Drinking orange juice is no healthier than eating a candy bar, by the way.) These same corporations and restaurants are also quick to displace blame on the very consumers they dupe when the inevitable health crises emerge. For instance, in 2013 McDonald's shut down their own employee website in part because in its health section it advised employees against eating the very kinds of unhealthy sugar, salt, and fat-laden foods the restaurant chain sells. (The website also offered advice on "tipping" which was clearly geared toward upward middle-class society and, concomitantly, cast light on the fact that McDonald's employees do not receive a living wage.)[2]

In a word, whitewashed superheroes, messiah figures, and the like operate as a kind of brain candy, encouraging us from birth to see these entities as embodiments of all that is wholesome, good, just, and loving in the world. The tooth fairy leaves money under our pillows, Santa delivers gifts to the "good" girls and boys, Superman saves the day, and a white messiah died on the cross to liberate us all from the devil and sin. What's more, the majority of villains and antichrist figures tend to be of a darker hue. (One need only peruse the "blackening" of said figures in Disney movies over the past century to confirm this reality.) These messages are packaged seductively in cartoons, picture books, blockbuster movies, magazines, and about every commercial medium imaginable. Even black folks internalize these messages (oftentimes despite ourselves) because we have been conditioned to see them as universal and morally transcendent. This phenomenon of conditioning is hardly new. In fact, it has been around for centuries—a direct outgrowth of Western imperialism.

What is new is the rise of postracial thinking and an attendant white social panic, resentment, and rage that encourages whites to see even the modest gains of the Civil Rights Movement as antiwhite and themselves as an oppressed majority. What postracial thinking does, above all else, is to reinforce the Horatio Alger myth that hard work, focus, and ambition are all that is required for success and prosperity in the United States. Suffice it to say, the Horatio Alger myth operates from the faulty premise that we live in a meritocracy. Postracialism substantiates this myth but in a much more contextualized way. That is, postracialism makes explicit the implicit claim undergirding the Horatio Alger myth: that race does not matter in the achievement and merit game. As Adam Mansbach rightly observes, postracialism, at its core, perpetuates the idea that we live in a post*racist* society.[3] Thus, postracialism is an idea that ultimately benefits whites by suggesting that blacks are no longer entitled (as if they ever were) to see their current social and economic crises as a direct historical consequence of slavery and Jim Crow segregation. According to this postracial/ist mindset, to see "race" as a meaningful category in terms of self-determination and economic access is for blacks to be excuse makers and even reverse racists. We are all on equal footing at this point in time in history, say the postracialists, and thus we need to move forward in the spirit of self-determination and democracy. The problem with this ahistorical, postracial/ist position is rather glaring—namely, it insidiously ignores the historical social, political, and economic circumstances upon which our current racial and structural inequalities are premised. What being postracial/ist means for me, as a black man, is that my critiques of extant white supremacy will likely be received in the white public domain as highly suspicious, if not extreme. Complicating matters further, most whites have a vested interest in thinking of racism as an individual rather than an institutional phenomenon. Suffice it to say, exposing the dangers of whitewashed superheroes, messiah figures, and the like is to the postracialist an unnecessary, if not counterproductive, enterprise. In truth, the real danger—especially as it pertains to raising and educating black children—is ignoring the reach, tenacity, and seductiveness of postracialism/cism.

Santa Is White: Get Over It!

In her lighthearted but substantive 2014 blog post, "Santa Claus Should Not Be a White Man Anymore," journalist Aisha Harris discusses the white Santa myth and how it negatively impacted her racial consciousness as a child. She argues that casting Santa as white is problematic because he is presented to children as a universal messianic figure. Indeed, the whiteness of his identity as a universal messianic figure conveys a very old and dangerous idea that whiteness equals goodness and godliness. Being that the racial discourse of whiteness relies on the othering of blackness and nonwhiteness in general, white Santa's cultural capital as a divine figure relies parasitically on negating the possibility of a black or nonwhite Santa. This racial calculus is so much a part of our cultural DNA that nobody has to verbalize its ideological significance to children. Harris opines that such an obviously racialized and important mythical character has no place in a soon-to-be majority-minority country. Her solution is to recast Santa as a penguin, removing the issue of race from the cultural calculation altogether:

Making Santa Claus an animal rather than an old white male could spare millions of nonwhite kids the insecurity and shame that I remember from childhood. Whether you celebrate the holiday or not, Santa is one of the first iconic figures foisted upon you: He exists as an incredibly powerful image in the imaginations of children across the country (and beyond, of course). That this genial, jolly man can only be seen as white—and consequently, that a Santa of any other hue is merely a "joke" or a chance to trudge out racist stereotypes—helps perpetuate the whole "white-as-default" notion endemic to American culture (and, of course, not just American culture).[4]

Harris's modest tongue-in-cheek proposal was met with fiery rebuke from a number of mediums, the most visible being from Fox News journalist Megyn Kelly on her show, *The Kelly File*. Tellingly, Kelly assembled an all-white panel to "discuss" the issue. Not only did she fail to consider the need to invite any people of color to the table for the debate, including Harris, but, more crucially, she failed to comprehend how her universalizing of her all-white panel (they can speak for everybody) was a profound act of white privilege. Most striking about the discussion, beyond the fact that at least one of the panelists seemed to agree in principle with Harris's argument, was Kelly's postracialist arrogance. Not only did she misrepresent Harris's argument as an irresponsible act of political correctness, but she indicted her for politicizing Santa's race in ways that denied the historical reality of his racial/cultural background. But, as Harris reminds Kelly in a journalistic retort, "What Fox News Doesn't Understand about Santa Claus," the Santa of our current cultural imagination hardly resembles the Greek bishop Saint Nicholas upon which the myth is based: "[Saint Nicholas] did not have a workshop in the North Pole nor eight faithful reindeer. Santa as we know him today is the result of wild imaginations and creative input from many people across centuries, including . . . Washington Irving and Clement Clark

Moore. He's utterly divorced from his religious and historical roots."[5] Further, as Harris reiterates several times in her essay, "Santa is a myth," meaning above all that he is a social construction that carries significant political capital. To discuss Santa as a historical figure rather than as the racialized mythical figure he is, then, obscures the racial agenda that makes whiteness so crucial to his identity. Naturalizing his whiteness (that is, making whiteness universal and invisible) also operates politically to make legitimate and necessary challenges to white supremacy appear inflammatory and polemical.

Kelly exhibited this ideological impulse to naturalize white supremacy when she prefaced the entire discussion with a message to her (white) viewers: "For you kids watching at home, Santa just is white. But this person [Harris] is arguing that maybe we should also have a black Santa."[6] Notwithstanding the fact that Harris's argument was *not* about replacing white Santa with a black one but about deracializing the myth altogether, Kelly inexplicably treats the idea of a black Santa as traumatizing to white children. In a remarkable critique of Kelly's thinly veiled *racist* postracialist mindset, comedian Jon Stewart on the *Daily Show* quipped, "'And who [is Megyn Kelly] actually talking to [when she declared that Santa is white]? Children who are sophisticated enough to be watching a news channel at 10 o'clock at night, yet innocent enough to still believe that Santa Claus is real; yet racist enough to be freaked out if he isn't white?'"[7]

What's really at stake for Kelly and the gatekeepers of white supremacist notions of divinity is just that—maintaining the superiority of whiteness. It should not come as a surprise, then, that Kelly extends her defense of Santa remaining white as historical fact with the historically inaccurate view that the Judeo-Christian historic figure Jesus Christ was white as well. Notably, because of the media backlash that her comments received, she modified her statement about Jesus's racial background, noting that she had learned, since her comments went public, that the issue of Jesus's "race" is "far from settled." Rather than acknowledge the problems of her racialism, though, Kelly opined that her controversial comments about Santa's race to children were tongue-and-cheek and that race baiters, including Aisha Harris, had blown her statements out of proportion. Once again, the gatekeepers of power and white privilege were crying victim when their efforts to maintain their power and privilege (which they are not seriously at risk of losing any time soon) were momentarily exposed. Lost in this brouhaha was the real and most pressing issue—black children continue to have to contend with messages via myths (religious and otherwise), cartoons, and cultural narratives that celebrate/elevate whiteness and denigrate/criminalize blackness.[8]

Nurture Shock and the Black Community

And, here, I want to turn critical attention to Po Bronson and Ashley Merryman's best-selling book *Nurture Shock*, not only because it provides useful insights into how certain white myths, like Santa Claus, impact racial consciousness, but also because of the way it undermines its own critique via romanticized notions about racial progress. This book is also noteworthy because it was published in 2009, toward the beginning of Barack Obama's first term as the first African American president and when postracialist thinking was arguably at its peak within and beyond black spaces. But first the useful insights *Nurture Shock* brings to light: The most striking revelation in the book for most readers, especially whites, was that school desegregation—one of the signature social outcomes of the Civil Rights Movement—did not neutralize white racism or improve race relations between whites and nonwhites. To the contrary, in fact. Indeed, what Bronson and Merryman expose, via several prominent studies that investigate the various ways babies, toddlers, adolescents, and teenagers develop and negotiate racial consciousness, is that the overwhelming majority of white children who go to racially diverse schools harbor far more racist attitudes than do whites who go to predominantly white schools. While Bronson and Merryman never explicitly use the term "white supremacy," their chapter on race and children is fundamentally about why said notion remains so difficult to explode even in the twenty-first century when most overt forms of racial discrimination have been eliminated.

A particularly startling discovery is that racial and racist attitudes are developed at a very early age and despite whether a parent chooses to discuss the issues. What certainly came as a "shock" to me was learning that even babies are aware of racial difference. Studies on race involving babies demonstrate, for instance, that they tend to stare at faces longer that are not racially familiar to them—the reason being that they are trying cognitively to reconcile the pigmentation and feature differences in the unfamiliar faces with those they see on a consistent basis. (In 2009 Bronson and Merryman sensationalized this little-known scholarship—no doubt as a marketing ploy—by titling their cover story for

Newsweek, "Is Your Baby Racist?") Substantiating Robert Jensen's argument in "White Privilege Shapes the U.S." that the ultimate white privilege is "the privilege to acknowledge you have unearned privilege but ignore what it means,"[9] Bronson and Merryman discovered that most whites—including the most politically conscientious—thought that *not* talking about race or racial difference was the best way to encourage their children to have antiracist mindsets. This is a deeply flawed strategy, according to Bronson and Merryman, because rather than communicate a message of racial equality, parental silence on race creates the impression for the children that race is a taboo topic of discussion. Moreover, it forces the children to rely on status quo reinforcing institutions in and beyond their social networks for their racial cues. Given that children "are active [rather than passive] constructors of knowledge,"[10] the white children that lacked parental intervention tended to align their racial attitudes with the status quo of normative whiteness. What this meant in regards to white children that attended racially diverse schools was increased opportunities to learn stereotypes and to reject nonwhite students.

As for how this dynamic influences the mindset and academic achievement of African American children, Bronson and Merryman explain—using April Harris-Britt's research on racial identity and child development—that the children who fare best in such a radically raced environment are those whose parents/guardians equip them mentally with both "preparation-for-bias" and "ethnic pride." That is, the parents alert their children to the fact that racism exists and will most likely have a negative impact on their lives, but they also stress the importance of being proud of their African American heritage against the socioeconomic obstacles of racism. These children tended to be "more engaged in school and more likely to attribute their success to their effort and ability."[11] Children with parents who emphasized the former over the latter, however, "were significantly less likely to connect their successes to effort, and much more likely to blame their failures on their teachers—whom they saw as biased against them."[12]

More striking to me than these findings—which I will expound upon in a moment—was the black Santa Claus experiment that Bronson and Merryman discuss at the close of their chapter. Intended, at once, to demonstrate how racially aware children are by the time they are six years old and to project hopeful solutions for combating racially biased attitudes for future generations, the closing pages offer more cause for concern than for hope. The gist of the study is this: During the Christmas holiday season, two racially diverse first-grade classes were read *Twas the Night B'fore Christmas* (1996)—Melodye Rosales' Afrocentric recasting of Clement C. Moore's classic Eurocentric tale—to test their racial reactions. After hearing the Afrocentric version—replete with an African American Santa Claus— the children began to discuss the racial components of the story without any prompting. Most of the white children rejected the idea out of hand, though several modified their views slightly throughout the week-long experiment, allowing for the ideas that black Santa might be white Santa's helper or cousin. The experiment culminated in the actual appearance of a black Santa at the end of the week.

As might be expected, the physical appearance of black Santa amplified the racial discussion. Bronson and Merryman report that the black children were "exultant" about black Santa Claus's arrival because it "proved [presumably to the white kids as much as to themselves] that Santa was black."[13] Faced with the material reality of a black Santa, the white children were thrown into a bit of a crisis. A few handled the crisis by trying directly to "discredit" black Santa by calling attention to his "thin" frame or invoking encounters with the "real" white Santa in other venues like K-Mart. The overwhelming majority of them, however, resolved this crisis—not by abandoning the white Santa idea—but by intensifying their effort to fit the black Santa into the dominant narrative as a "sidekick" or special helper of some kind. What struck a personal emotional chord with me as a father was the authors' depiction of Brent, a rather outspoken black boy in the classroom whose spirited responses reminded me of my son Elijah. Whereas most of the children are passive in the presence of black Santa Claus, Brent confronts him openly and aggressively, remarking "There ain't no black Santas!"[14] When the black Santa asks Brent "what color do you see?" Brent responds incredulously, "Black—but under your socks you might not be!"[15] Only after black Santa pulls up his pant leg, revealing black ankles, does Brent finally believe. He bellows enthusiastically, "This is a black Santa! . . . He's got black skin and his black boots are like the white Santa's boots."[16]

After chronicling Brent's celebration, the authors tell us that despite black Santa's visit to class, *all* the children depicted Santa as "snowy-white" when later they were asked to draw a portrait of him on paper. No doubt trying to end the chapter on a high note, Bronson and Merryman relay that "the shock of the Santa storybook did allow the children to start talking about race in a way that had never before occurred to them. And their questions started a year-long dialogue about race issues."[17] They then add a rather curious example of how this dialogue erupted into a heightened racial awareness across racial lines. In a history lesson on the Civil Rights Movement that highlighted African Americans' experiences, "both a black and a white child noticed that white people were nowhere to be found in the story, and, troubled, they decided to find out just where in history both peoples were."[18]

Though Bronson and Merryman usefully upset many common (white) assumptions about the benefits of desegregation in schools, their decidedly rosy closing narrative—most especially their lighthearted rendering of Brent's reaction to black Santa—was very distressing. Weren't the ostensible aims of the chapter to highlight the (white) impulse to romanticize racial progress narratives and to expose how white silence on race and racism perpetuates rather than challenges the status quo of racial inequality? That Brent feels emboldened to verbally attack black Santa—who is also consequently an adult—on the ideological basis of white supremacy is for me the most "shocking" and disturbing aspect of this narration. That is, Brent has so deeply internalized white supremacy that he becomes quite literally a racial policing force. Rather than feel optimistic that Brent's (inappropriate) interrogation of black Santa ends with a feeling of racial validation—as the narration of the scene clearly encourages the readers to do—I was mortified by the social and emotional implications of his behavior. In a mere six years, Brent had learned, in effect, to devalue blackness and, by extension, himself. To wit, this was the insidious ideological monster that corrupted my vision of the world and against which my progressive black parenting strategies were aimed at dismantling. Would someone run interference for Brent as I and my children's mother try to do for our children and help him unlearn normative whiteness before he, like so many countless other black boys, begins to lose his way in school and in society at large?

There's always hope, I kept telling myself, even though deep down I knew the odds were not in his favor. The rosy ending of the chapter—which lauds as a breakthrough the children's awareness that whites were missing from the Civil Rights narrative—encapsulates my cause for concern. As Bronson and Merryman make note of earlier in the chapter, white children do not need formalized messages of race pride as African Americans do because "they naturally decipher [at an early age] that they belong to the race that has more power, wealth, and control in society"—an awareness that fosters feelings of security and confidence. Suffice it to say, then, that there is nothing terribly "shocking" about the children's awareness that whites were missing from this decidedly *atypical* Afrocentric rendering of the Civil Rights Movement. (So far removed was the discussion of African American experiences from the curriculum in my secondary education that it never dawned on me until after I was exposed to African American studies in college that African Americans were prominent players in American history.) Following Bronson and Merryman's own logic here, a true breakthrough would have entailed the children noticing the absence of African Americans and Native Americans in, say, historical narratives about the Civil War or the signing of the Declaration of Independence. That the authors appear oblivious to this salient contradiction highlights in rather dramatic fashion the tenacity of the white supremacist discourse (my term not theirs) that they map in their chapter.

Even though my children's mother and I are acutely aware of and responsive to these racial dynamics and the intellectual and emotional havoc they can wreak on African American children's self-confidence and emotional stability, we remain on our collective heels in trying to keep our children protected from these insidious obstacles. I spoke to this phenomenon in *Blinded by the Whites* as it pertained to parenting my daughter, whose self-esteem and notions of black women's beauty were profoundly impacted by pervasive images of white beauty rendered through commercial mediums from Disney films to Barbie dolls. At the age of four, my daughter became preoccupied with the age-old children's story *Goldilocks* and, for a time, began to identify black folks, including her parents, on the basis of skin tone and even hair texture. These perspectives were directly at odds with those she was receiving at home. Which is to say her environment outside the home and, no doubt, her exposure to these perspectives on television, movies, and popular media in general trumped our teachings at home. What I came to realize was that we had to be aggressively proactive in educating our children to love themselves and appreciate their cultural heritage, including their African ancestry. I bought my daughter a virtual library of books on black/brown girls which celebrated and usefully critiqued extant dynamics of colorism. As a family, we watched the illuminating documentary "Dark Girls" and, afterward, discussed the extent to which skin pigmentation, hair, and facial features continue to inform our race-gender-class realities. My daughter, who was eight at the time, and son, who was eleven, were able to engage with said issues at a high critical level. Indeed, they were able to apply some of the critical models introduced in the documentary to their lived experience.

Yet and still, several months later my daughter made a judgmental comment to her brother about how "black" and "dark" one of her school peers was. I overheard them discussing the issue—or rather I overheard my son schooling his little sister to be exact—about the problems of such colorist language. By the time I intervened, my daughter was already owning up to her colorism. When I expressed my dismay and disappointment, she began to tear up. Her exact words were, "Does this make me a bad person, daddy?" I responded by saying that the issue was not about being "bad" or "good" but about becoming self-aware of how internalized white supremacy manifests itself in how we privilege certain Eurocentric features and devalue Afrocentric ones. I'm reminded here of Zora Neale Hurston's quip about colorism in her highly controversial autobiography *Dust Track on a Road*: "I saw no benefit in excusing my looks by claiming to be half Indian. In fact, I boast that I am the only Negro in the United States whose grandfather on the mother's side was *not* an Indian chief."[19] Though raised in an all-black and fiercely proud community that routinely bucked white power, Hurston (who was of a lighter hue) still couldn't escape the ideological messaging of colorism.[20] Then as now, white- and light-skin beauty was treated as self-evident, relegating dark girls to the ideological basement of beauty politics and elevating "light-skinned girls" in ways that, more often than not, made them targets of sexual conquest and exoticism across racial lines. I remember taking my children to Disney Land when my daughter was four and my son eight and being mortified by the sight of black and brown girls dressed as white princesses. (This was, of course, before the lone black princess in Disney lore, Tiana from the "Princess and the Frog," was created.) The uncritical celebration of white beauty on display at Disney—which, again, depends parasitically on the erasure/denigration of black beauty—was nauseating.

The key point here is that celebrating white beauty—which Disney does better than any other social medium that I can think of beyond, say, its partner-in-crime Hollywood—means by default denigrating Afrocentric beauty. Our recent cultural infatuation with the stunningly beautiful talent Lupita Nyong'o (whose riveting performance as the slave Patsey in "12 Years a Slave" earned her an Oscar Award in 2014 and catapulted her to stardom) is not so much an indication that white America's cultural tastes have changed, but rather that there is, and has always been, "space" within the "rules" of white beauty for "exceptions" (think Iman, Naomi Campbell, and Grace Jones). One need only ask Nyong'o herself, who openly admitted to fighting against a discourse of self-hate since childhood because of her Afrocentric features:

I remember a time when I too felt unbeautiful. I put on the TV and only saw pale skin. I got teased and taunted about my night-shaded skin. And my one prayer to God, the miracle worker, was that I would wake up lighter-skinned. The morning would come and I would be so excited about seeing my new skin that I would refuse to look down at myself until I was in front of a mirror because I wanted to see my fair face first. And every day I experienced the same disappointment of being just as dark as I had been the day before. I tried to negotiate with God: I told him I would stop stealing sugar cubes at night if he gave me what I wanted; I would listen to my mother's every word and never lose my school sweater again if he just made me a little lighter. But I guess God was unimpressed with my bargaining chips because He never listened.[21]

It is important to note that Nyong'o was only thirty-one when she gave this speech. She is not speaking from the standpoint of a seventy-one-year-old civil rights activist. What is so troubling about her insights (which took guts to verbalize given the real risks to her career) is indeed how similar they *would be* to those of a seventy-year-old civil rights activist. To underscore the tenacity of what Nyong'o calls the "seduction of [racial] inadequacy," it is important to call attention to the reality of her giftedness on multiple levels. The daughter of a college professor, she is not only stunningly beautiful and talented, she was also a top-notch student, completing a bachelor's degree from Hampshire College and master's degree in acting from the Yale School of Drama. It would seem that if anybody could avoid the pernicious effects of racial stigmas it would be Nyong'o. Her emotional vulnerability to these white supremacist messages of beauty, intelligence, and social value underscores why the fight to be recognized as fully human in the United States and the world over, to some degree, is far from over.

My daughter's impulse to be Goldilocks at four years old derives from a similar set of racial messages that being Afrocentric in appearance, and particularly having dark skin and kinky hair, is unattractive and even primitive. Consider this case in point. My daughter was wearing an Afro style in the summer of 2014 when a ten-year-old Latina playmate commented that her hair looked "ghetto" and that she was instructed by her mother not to play with "ghetto" children. The wicked irony was that the Latino girl was living with her mother's friend at the time after being forced to move because of financial challenges. In other words, the prospects of living in the ghetto were extremely high for her and virtually nonexistent for my daughter. Yet, she felt empowered (seemingly through the influence of her mother) to lash out at my daughter and associate her natural hair texture with undesirability and primitivism. The silver lining is that my son Elijah and a host of kids on the block, including Latinas, Jamaicans, and even whites, came to my daughter's defense and the offending child was compelled via peer pressure to apologize. Nevertheless, my daughter's self-esteem took a hit. Though she has been hyperaware of her appearance for as long as I can remember (which is sadly the reality of many girls across racial lines), she has since the incident become increasingly more self-conscious about wearing her hair in an Afro style. Though we discussed the matter extensively as a family and Octavia was able to articulate why the problem was not her hairstyle but the twisted racial politics of her peer, it was clear to me that Octavia was still reeling emotionally from the insult, that the racial shaming had a lasting toxic effect. Of course, the insult was one among countless others that my daughter has witnessed firsthand since birth. And therein lies the challenge: though my daughter had a critical model against which to critique her friend's white supremacist logic along with a familial network of support, her brown peer-assailant (who, as a Latina, is hardly exempt from xenophobia or racial othering) wielded the cultural capital of white supremacy. Even our best-trained and most-supported black children are susceptible to belittling of this kind. It should go without saying that if blacks with resources and strong support networks are still vulnerable to assaults on their personhood and physical features, then blacks who lack such resources and support networks do not stand much of a chance.

The sad reality is that I am all too familiar with the source of my daughter's cultural shame and shaming. As a child growing up in the 1970s and 1980s, I have vivid memories of Buckwheat from the popular TV series "The Little Rascals," nigger Jim from Mark Twain's *Huckleberry Finn*, the primitive "Africans" from the Tarzan series, and, of course, the countless big-lipped, broad-nosed buffoons and Africanized cartoons from Disney movies to the Tom and Jerry cartoon series. As children we internalized these images and the shame that they were inevitably designed to foster. To be called an "African," "jungle bunny," or even "Kunta Kinte" (the Gambian-born American slave and focal point of the 1970s mini-series "Roots") in my day was only slightly less insulting than someone disparaging your mother. Indeed, I witnessed and participated in several fights that stemmed from such insults. The racial propaganda mediums, including network TV, Hollywood, the mainstream media, state and federal government agencies, the judicial and police departments, and secondary educational institutions, were wickedly successful at making Africa and Africans synonymous in our cultural imaginations with primitivism, anti-intellectualism, hypersexuality, disease, political corruption, and the like. The unspoken narrative that many of us had also internalized was that, however horrendous was slavery (which we had little to no knowledge of given that it was taboo and dangerous to discuss openly and conspicuously omitted from our formal educational process), our "forced migration" as slaves to the West and Eurocentric civilization was ultimately beneficial. This is not to say, of course, that there weren't competing notions available, among them pro-black and nationalist ideas that tried to flip the script of white supremacist propaganda and celebrate Africa as the mother of civilization (which, of course, it is) and re-script enslaved blacks and descendants as kings and queens (which the majority of them were not). But in many cases, the federal government actively and aggressively infiltrated many of the groups that were challenging white supremacist ideology, from the iconic SCLC (Southern Christian Leadership Conference), to which Martin Luther King Jr. was closely aligned, to the Black Panthers and The Nation of Islam, to which Malcolm X was closely aligned. Moreover, even to the degree to which these pro-black ideas were effective in challenging white supremacist ideology, they often reproduced male-centric and hypermasculine notions of blackness that reified as much as challenged status quo notions of domination.[22] To this day, the idea of Africa (which happens to be a continent, not a country, and also happens to include Egypt) remains othered in our racialized political consciousness. Though, say, Ghanaians are as different culturally from Nigerians as the French are from the Russians, we have been conditioned as US citizens to see Africa and Africans as monolithic. Indeed, many blacks—past and present—internalized these ideas of a monolithic Africa to the point of actually believing that they would find instant kinship with indigenous Africans upon returning to the continent. Anecdotally speaking, what African Americans often discovered when they returned to parts of Africa was just how profoundly "American" they were culturally.

If we take seriously the intensity and insidiousness of the white supremacist messaging that is rendered through fairy tales, mythologies, cartoons, and even religion in the United States, it should become clear that we cannot rid our society of racial inequality if we cannot rid ourselves of the cultural mediums that reproduce and substantiate it. As this chapter has sought to reveal, there is nothing random or innocent about this whitewashing phenomenon. Santa Claus and the Judeo-Christian messiah figure Jesus are constructed as white for specific political and ideological purposes, the chief one being to reinforce the idea that whiteness is superior, divine, and spiritually transcendent. The fact that these white-messiah figures remain dominant fixtures in our society and that folks who dare to challenge their racial validity, like Aisha Harris, are maligned as radical or even racist is telling indeed. In his tour de force *Between the World and Me* Ta-Nehisi Coates asserts, "race is the child of racism, not the father."[23] His point is that race was invented to facilitate the domination of one group over another. Thus, we cannot put an end to racism until we truly explode the concept of race in all its various and complex iterations. This does not mean striving to be colorblind in a white supremacist society for doing so only covers up racial inequalities; it means actively striving to dismantle white supremacist mindsets and institutions. To be sure, we will know that we're heading in the right direction when our society no longer seeks to whitewash religious and mythical figures; when doing so is deemed as taboo as burning witches is in our current society. The world of fantasy should not be the dominant domain of whiteness; Disneyland should not be a hallmark of white superiority with smatterings of token racial representation. Ideologically speaking, whiteness masquerades as universal; tries to occupy the domain of normalcy. So what we witness in these whitewashed mythologies, fairy tales, and spiritual figures is a dangerous form of racial propaganda. Given this reality, it should come as no surprise that most whites find it easy to dismiss black pain or own their culpability in black suffering—past and present—and, concomitantly, to demonize even unarmed black children, like Tamir Rice and Trayvon Martin, to name but a few, who have been senselessly murdered at the hands of white cops and community police. Even as we have made significant strides in our society in terms of identifying the problems of this racial propaganda (Megyn Kelly did, after all, get taken to task for her whitewashing of Santa Claus and Jesus and was pressed, as a result, to backtrack on many of her racist criticisms of Harris) we have a long way to go yet. What our whitewashed mythologies, fairy tales, and spiritual figures propagate is that the good guys are always cloaked in white (skin) and the bad guys are always cloaked in black or dark (skin). History shows us something quite different; that whites have long participated in and tried to whitewash or erase their unspeakable acts of cruelty and domination against blacks and people of color in the United States. These whitewashed fairy tales, mythologies, and spiritual figures are so dangerous precisely because they obscure this reality and encourage us to see the chief victims of white supremacy in blacks, indigenous Americans, and Chicanos as criminals, social parasites, and moral degenerates and whites as liberators, saviors, or even victims of racial hate. The time to abandon this racial propaganda has come. In fact, it is long past due.

Coda

I was sitting in my doctor's office waiting to be seen when news of Dylan Roof's capture flashed across my cellphone screen. On June 17, 2015, Roof walked into a prayer service at Emanuel African Methodist Episcopal Church in Charleston, South Carolina, and slaughtered nine African Americans. The diabolical deed was done immediately after the black congregants welcomed him into their prayer circle. An avowed white supremacist who openly expressed his racial hatred on social media, Roof plotted to use the racial mass murder to start a race war. Originally intending to take his own life to avoid prosecution, he intentionally left one of the congregants alive so that she could bear witness to his racist agenda.

When I saw the news that Roof was apprehended I was flooded with intense emotion. I was at once relieved that he had been brought to justice and would be forced to stand trial, terrified at the racial implications of his hate crime (could there be copycats?), and overwhelmed by feelings of helplessness. After all, George Zimmerman stalked and murdered an innocent black teenager in Trayvon Martin and not only avoided prosecution but became a hero in white nationalist circles. Moreover, President Donald Trump, who has an ugly track record of racial hatemongering and discrimination, strongly endorses the unconstitutional police program "Stop and Frisk" despite the fact that racial profiling within police departments is rampant in our society and police officers are ostensibly licensed to kill blacks as the abysmally low prosecution rates of killer cops reveal.

When my surgeon Tom (not his real name) walked into my room I was literally on the verge of tears. A late-sixty-something white male with a warm smile and genial disposition, Tom teaches at the University of Miami's medical school and is world-renowned in his field. Tom had performed a minor elective surgical procedure on me three weeks prior and I was returning for a routine checkup to make sure I was healing properly. Tom and I had hit it off immediately in our initial meeting as we both shared the commonality of being UM professors and had similar tastes in food, art, and cinema. More importantly, he was a caring and compassionate human being, which is likely why he was so beloved in his field beyond his renowned surgical prowess. Tom immediately recognized my intense emotional disposition and asked if everything was okay. "They've just apprehended Dylan Roof," I said breathlessly. "Dylan who?" Tom asked earnestly. "Dylan Roof. The terrorist who killed those black church folks in South Carolina." "Ah yes," he replied, recalling the event. "That guy has some serious mental health problems, right? But I would hardly consider him a terrorist. A madman certainly but not a terrorist."

Because most whites I have encountered in my adult life, including many self-identified liberals and antiracists, have exhibited serious blind spots when it comes to engaging with issues of race and racism, I am rarely caught off-guard in such discussions. As I've mentioned, my previous encounters with Tom had been pleasant. Though we never discussed issues of race or racism, he seemed like the type of informed white person that one could talk with about such sensitive matters. He wasn't. More critically, I had let my guard down so I was emotionally unprepared for his profoundly uncritical analysis of Roof's terrorist mindset and motives. When I opened my mouth to speak, I realized that I was not only angry but also hurt by his paternalistic tone and self-assurance: "How on earth can you say Dylan Roof is not a terrorist? He set out to start a race war by randomly killing innocent black folks and in a church service no less. He is as much a terrorist as the Klansmen who bombed Sixteenth Street Baptist Church in Birmingham Alabama in 1963 and killed those four little girls. Those white men weren't mentally challenged; just boiling over with racist hate." Seemingly nonplussed, Tom averred paternalistically, "All of that may be true to some degree I guess, David, but only a madman would do such a heinous thing; wouldn't you agree? Besides, the *real* terrorists are radical Islamists. They kill with impunity. They are truly heartless."

I was completely dumbfounded. Here was a scholar of medicine, science, and reason, diagnosing Roof as mentally ill without a sliver of empirical evidence to support his claim. Indeed, Roof had just been apprehended. At the time, very little was known about Roof, including his mental health. (Since his apprehension, he has not only been deemed mentally competent to stand trial but convicted on all thirty-three counts of federal hate crimes he faced for his murdering spree.) But facts and logic have always been irrelevant within white supremacist ideology. Or, more accurately, they are relevant and valued only to the extent to which they reinforce status quo white supremacist thinking. Tom and many well-meaning whites were not interested in the facts of the case or in getting to the bottom of Dylan's racial motivations. In truth, many are all too familiar with Dylan's racist mindset and motivations and the long and bloody history of white-on-black terrorism in this country. More to the point, Tom was evaluating Roof's character and state of mind vis-à-vis a white supremacist lens. Read through this lens, Roof was not a terrorist, regardless of the circumstances, because he was a white, Christian man and his victims were African Americans. Indeed, the armchair diagnosis of mental insanity offered Tom and many white apologists a convenient way to distinguish Roof's terrorist mindset and lethal racist behavior from "ordinary" whites folks like themselves and the long-standing practice of white-on-black terrorism in America. Dylan was crazy. His actions were that of a racist madman. He was an outlier; a renegade; in no way representative of how most whites feel about their black peers and fellow citizens.

Though Tom never uttered the words race or racism in our debate, it was clear he associated terrorism with Islamic people of color and specifically brown Middle Easterners. Within this raced calculation, the true victims of terrorism by racial default were "innocent" (white) Americans. Thus, the very idea that a white man could be a terrorist struck him as twisted, if not outright unfathomable. This dynamic was nowhere clearer than in the ridiculous debate around the confederate flag that Roof's racial murdering spree ignited. Roof displayed the confederate flag in several of his racist social media posts—a flag that was still being flown at the statehouse in South Carolina at the time of his killing and that is prominently featured within the official Mississippi state flag to this day. Even as there is no disputing that the one-time battle flag of the confederacy is affiliated with the KKK and other hate groups in the modern era and that "Dixiecrats" adapted it in the 1960s as a symbol of white supremacy in direct opposition to the Civil Rights Movement and attendant civil rights legislation within the Democratic Party, white South Carolinians and whites in the country at large continue to view the flag as a symbol of southern pride rather than racism. According to a CNN/ORC poll taken just days after the South Carolina legislature voted overwhelmingly on June 9, 2015, to remove the flag from statehouse grounds, an astounding 57 percent of white participants felt the confederate flag represented southern pride as compared to only 33 percent who felt it represented racial hate. Black views diverged significantly: 72 percent viewed the flag as representative of racial hate while only 17 percent believed it represented southern pride. (Also worth noting, a whopping 61 percent of whites did not view the killing spree as an act of terrorism.) [1] To be sure, even if Roof, a high school dropout, didn't fully comprehend the history of the confederate flag, he certainly understood its cultural messages of white supremacy and racial terrorism. Though in the end the flag did come down in South Carolina,[2] the issue of the flag's symbolic representation remains hotly contentious, especially within white southern communities. It should come as no surprise then that pro-confederate-flag activists have consistently denied the racist/terrorist history the flag embodies or been gleefully oblivious or uncaring of how that history impacts African American communities. To signify on an old political adage, white supremacy never lets the facts get in the way of a good story about southern pride and protecting "states rights" and (white) self-determination.

Suffice it to say, I processed Tom's racialist rationale to distinguish Roof's racist mentality/behavior from white identity in an instant and surmised that flight instead of fight was the healthiest course of action. What I understand from experience is that racial debates of this nature have relatively low emotional stakes for many whites of Tom's professional and social ilk; that continuing the debate would have likely only raised my blood pressure and stress level. When I got up to leave, Tom—no doubt sensing my intense frustration and discomfort—tried to defuse the situation: "My deepest apologies, David. These are trying times for us all. We can certainly agree that the senseless killing of innocent people is reprehensible. Anyway, you're here to get a checkup. Let's concentrate on the business at hand." I complied, if only because rescheduling would have been a major headache and Tom realized from my reaction that it was best to end the debate.

To be clear, I am absolutely certain that Tom repudiated Dylan Roof's racist killing spree and had no overt racial agenda when discussing his views of terrorism. The problem, in fact, is that Tom *was* being sincere. However genuine and heartfelt were his insights, they were premised ideologically on white supremacy. To invoke James Baldwin once more, it was Tom's "innocence which constitute[d] the crime."[3] White supremacy has been normalized to the extent to which racist or racialized notions function culturally as a kind of racial commonsense. I had mentioned earlier that I bailed on the discussion with Tom because the stakes were so radically different for him and me. The racial commonsense/white supremacist lens through which he evaluated Roof's terrorist behavior is culturally and racially affirming for him as a white man. Culturally speaking, whites as a collective epitomize moral fortitude, equality, liberty, and justice. They are the saviors of the world, the gatekeepers of all things sacred and holy, and champions of the innocent, weak and dispossessed. In other words, they are the polar *opposite* of terrorists. Or rather, I should say, the polar opposite of how white Americans and Westerners in general conceptualize brown Middle Eastern terrorists as heartless religious fanatical monsters who prey on the weak—a conceptualization that conspicuously ignores how Christianity and white supremacy has been employed for centuries in the United States to exploit, dominate, enslave, and murder generations of people of color, especially people of African descent. This white supremacist lens allows, on the one hand, for whites to view homegrown white supremacist terrorists and hate groups as radical and out of step with mainstream white America's attitudes toward racial equality and, on the other hand, to view brown radical Islamist terrorists as representative of Middle Eastern culture and Islamic religious tradition. A similar version of this white supremacist lens was at play in the 1960s when the most significant Civil Rights crusader of our time, Martin Luther King Jr., was tagged as a kind of terrorist threat to the United States after his famed "I Have a Dream Speech" during the March on Washington in 1963. The notorious head of the FBI, J. Edgar Hoover, circulated a memo throughout the bureau declaring MLK as "the most dangerous Negro of the future of this nation."[4] King's true "threat" was challenging the established order of white supremacy—a challenge that made him a prime target for state- and federally sanctioned terrorism and surveillance and eventually led to his assassination.

Tom could confidently rehearse this white supremacist propaganda that separated out homegrown and long-standing white supremacist terrorism from radical Islamist terrorism because white supremacist thinking continues to inform and, in many instances, dictate how we understand and experience our social, cultural, and political realities. I found myself in the untenable position of having to challenge racial commonsense. The odds of my winning that debate were slim. Regardless of the outcome, the social reality was that black lives mattered significantly less than white lives and attaining justice for those nine human beings that Roof mercilessly slaughtered was far from guaranteed. For me, this ordeal was a matter of life and death. The relative ease with which many whites devalued the lives of those senselessly murdered African Americans revealed in no uncertain terms how they felt about the value of my life and those of my black friends and family. For Tom, the issue was largely trivial; Roof's fate would have little, if any, bearing on his privileged racial status as an upper-class professional white man. Our judicial and policing systems were designed explicitly to protect and serve people like him and to criminalize people like me. Roof's conviction or lack thereof in a court of law was not going to matter one way or another in terms of exploding white supremacist ideology or institutional dominance.

The key point of my anecdote is to underscore why the tropes under investigation in this book—lovable racists, magical negroes, and white messiahs—remain alive and well today. What I have attempted to do throughout this book is to identify the ways that white identity is parasitically bound up with black identity specifically and the identities of people of color in general. The tremendous emotional, cultural, social, political, and economic advantages that whites enjoy as a direct result of white supremacist ideology and institutions of power mean that there is very little incentive for whites to challenge the status quo. The tropes remain alive and well, then, because they help whites facilitate willful white ignorance. More specifically, these tropes constitute cultural buffers which afford whites the luxury of ignoring their racial privilege and the cost that blacks and people color incur as a direct and indirect result of it.

A chief goal of this book is to disrupt this white supremacist calculus: to shift the political dynamic of racial inequality so that whites are put in the uncomfortable position of having to defend their pathological investment in white supremacist ideology. White supremacy is most dangerous when it can avoid being named or identified. To invoke the iconic movie *Fight Club*, the first and second rule of white supremacy is "you do not talk about" white supremacy.[5] As exasperating as it may be at times to speak out on racism and white supremacy, it is critical that antiracist scholars within and beyond black spaces do so wherever and whenever we encounter it. Our silence is not only counterproductive to blacks'/people of color's plight of equality and justice; it renders us complicit on some level in white supremacist ideology and power. Indeed, white supremacy depends on this silence/complicity for survival. Which is precisely why we must now and always speak truth to power. To echo the words of radical black activist Assata Shakur, "We have nothing to lose but our chains."[6]

Notes

FOREWORD

1. Derrick Bell, *Faces at the Bottom of the Well: The Permanence of Racism* (New York: Basic, 1992), 47.
2. Nell Irvin Painter, *The History of White People* (New York: Norton, 2010), 30.

INTRODUCTION

1. Robin DiAngelo, "White Fragility: Why It's So Hard to Talk to White People about Racism." *TheGoodMenProject.com*, April 9, 2015, https://goodmenproject.com/featured-content /white-fragility-why-its-so-hard-to-talk-to-white-people-about -racism-twlm/.
2. Ibid.
3. Robin DiAngelo, "White Fragility," *International Journal of Critical Pedagogy* 3, no. 3 (2011): 54–70, 64.
4. Brit Bennett, "I Don't Know What to Do with Good White People," *Jezebel*, December 17, 2014, http://jezebel.com/i-dont -know-what-to-do-with-good-white-people-1671201391.
5. Eduardo Bonilla-Silva, *Racism without Racists: Color-Blind Racism and the Persistence of Racial Inequality in America* (Lanham, MD: Rowan & Littlefield, 2002), 15.
6. Ibid.
7. Ta-Nehisi Coates, "The Good Racist People," *New York Times*, March 6, 2013, http://www.nytimes.com/2013/03/07/opinion /coates-the-good-racist-people.html.
8. Ibid.
9. Ibid.
10. Rich Morin, "Crime Rises among Second-Generation Immi-grants as They Assimilate," Pewresearch.org, October 15,

2013, http://www.pewresearch.org/fact-tank/2013/10/15/crime-rises-among -second-generation-immigrants-as-they-assimilate.

11. Tessa Berensen, "Donald Trump's *Saturday Night Live* Protests Grows," *Times .com*, October 27, 2015, http://time.com/4089468/donald-trump-saturday -night-live-protests.

12. In 2013 the Supreme Court struck down Section 4 of the Voting Rights Act by a 5–4 vote. Section 4 designated that certain parts of the country—namely the South and states like Texas—that have historically obstructed blacks from voting need to have federal preclearance to change their voting procedures, such as requiring photo identifications to vote.

13. In 2008 John McCain received 55% of the white vote and Obama received 45%, which is within the percentage range that Democrat candidates have performed since Jimmy Carter was elected in 1977. In 2012 Mitt Romney received a whopping 59% of the white vote to Obama's 39%. In fact, Romney dominated every major white category, including women, men, and youth.

14. David C. Wilson, "The Elephant in the Exit Poll Results: Most White Women Supported Romney," *Huffington Post*, January 8, 2013, http://www.huffington post.com/david-c-wilson/the-elephant-in-the-exit_b_2094354.html.

15. James Baldwin, *The Fire Next Time* (New York: Random House, 1993), 22, my emphasis.

16. Toni Morrison, *Playing the Dark: Whiteness and the Literary Imagination* (New York: Random House, 1992), 20.

17. Ibid.

18. Baldwin, *The Fire Next Time*, 6.

19. Ibid., 8.

20. Tellingly, the intraracial bar of expectation for Barack Obama—the *real* first black president—was set even lower. As Martell Teasley and I note in *Nation of Cowards*, (*Nation of Cowards: Black Activism in Barack Obama's Post-Racial America* [Bloomington: Indiana University Press, 2012]), Obama ripped a page right out of Bill Clinton's political playbook for leveraging such cultural authenticity to gain black votes and support.

21. Melissa Harris-Perry, "The Clinton Fallacy: Did blacks really make big economic gains during the '90s?" *Slate*, January 24, 2008, http://www.slate.com /articles/news_and_politics/politics/2008/01/the_clinton_fallacy.html.

22. Ibid.

23. Derrick Bell, *Silent Covenants: Brown V. Board of Education and the Unfulfilled Hopes for Racial Reform* (New York: Oxford University Press, 2004), 78.

24. Edward Said, *Orientalism* (New York: Random House, 1994), 85.

CHAPTER ONE

1. Solomon Northup, *Twelve Years a Slave: Narrative of Solomon Northup*, introd. by Sue Lyles Eakin (Houston: Eakin Films and Publishing, 2013), 48–89, my emphasis.

2. His allegorical depiction of Mrs. Auld as a kind of Eve who is corrupted beyond redemption after being introduced to slavery by her husband is arguably his most salient attempt to distinguish among white slaveholders.
3. See Keith Byerman's *Remembering the Past in Contemporary African American Fiction*.
4. According to Sue Eakin, there is no hard evidence that Wilson even held antislavery views.
5. There was a 1984 television film based on a version of *Twelve Years* and entitled "Solomon Northup's Odyssey."
6. Solomon notes on several occasions how strong and capable the black women are as laborers. However, these representations of black women's strength do not typically extend beyond their physicality.
7. Ikard, *Blinded by the Whites: Why Race Still Matters in 21st-Century America* (Bloomington: Indiana University Press, 2013), 62–67.
8. Northup, *Twelve Years A Slave*, 86–87.
9. Mr. Hughes in Douglass's *Narrative* derives a similar form of cultural capital when he "allows" Douglass to keep a tiny fraction of the wages he earns for Hughes working in the shipyards in Baltimore.
10. Northup, *Twelve Years A Slave*, 57.
11. Ibid., 52.
12. Ibid., 59.
13. Ibid.
14. Ibid., 117.
15. Ibid., 110.
16. Ibid.
17. Iconic black feminist scholar bell hooks is one of the film's most outspoken critics. In an interview with Melissa Harris-Perry she panned the film, arguing that its portrayal of black women only gives "expression to the black male feeling." Though acknowledging that there is "much to praise" about the film, scholar-activist Carol Boyce Davies also finds wanting its portrayal of the women and black resistance in general. On *theguardian.com* she argues that the film did not remain true to the slave narrative, which highlighted many instances of slave resistance and revolt, including by black women.
18. In a "Wire.com" interview Alice Walker listed the movie on her conspiracy-filled "Best of 2013" List.
19. John Ridley, *12 Years a Slave*. DVD. Directed by Steve McQueen. Miami: Fox, 2013. All the quotes in this section derive from the movie.
20. See Saidiya V. Hartman's *Scenes of Subjection: Terror, Slavery, and Self-Making in Nineteenth-Century America*.
21. Zora Neale Hurston, *Their Eyes Were Watching God* (New York: Harper & Row, 1990), 12.
22. Ridley, *12 Years*.
23. Edward P. Jones, *The Known World* (New York: Amistad, 2003), 64.

CHAPTER TWO

1. Toni Morrison, *Beloved* (New York: Penguin, 1987), 180.
2. Ibid.
3. As David Zirin notes in "Florida State Seminoles: The Champions of Racist Mascots," FSU routinely and inaccurately touts that it has the backing of the Seminole Nation to use the Seminole as a mascot. In reality, FSU has only the backing of the Seminole Tribal Council in Florida, which numbers only about three thousand and has a substantial financial investment in the branding of tribe in the state. The overwhelming majority of Seminoles that make up the Seminole Nation reside in Oklahoma and they have repeatedly expressed their vehement objection to the use of the Seminole and other Native American tribes as mascots.
4. Toni Morrison, *Playing in the Dark* (New York: Random House, 1992), 15.
5. See my *Blinded by the Whites*.
6. Susan Candiotti and Dana Ford. "Connecticut school victims were shot multiple times," *CNN*, December 16, 2012, http://www.cnn.com/2012/12/15/us/connecticut-school-shooting.
7. Melissa Harris-Lacewell (now Harris-Perry), "'Do You Know What It Means . . . ?': Mapping Emotion in the Aftermath of Katrina," in *Seeking Higher Ground: The Hurricane Katrina Crisis, Race, and Public Policy Reader*, ed. Kristen Clarke and Manning Marable (New York: Palgrave Macmillan, 2007), 153–72.
8. "A Concert for Hurricane Relief" hosted by Matt Lauer. NBC, September 2 2005.
9. Harris-Lacewell, "'Do You Know What It Means . . . ,'" 167.
10. "107 children, youth and young adults killed in Chicago in one year." AustinTalks, May 25, 2012, http://austintalks.org/2012/05/107-children-youth-young-adults-killed-in-chicago-in-one-year.
11. David Sirota, "Time to Profile White Men?" *Salon.com*. Monday, December 17, 2012, http://www.salon.com/2012/12/17/would_the_u_s_government_profile_white_men.
12. I put the word "white" in parentheses to underscore that this popular notion about children being blameless is racially parasitical in the ways we have previously discussed.
13. For insightful discussion of this controversy, see Brittany Cooper's essay "White Supremacy Wins Again: Melissa Harris Perry and the Racial False Equivalence," in *Salon.com*.
14. James Baldwin, *"Everybody's Protest Novel,"* in *Baldwin: Collected Essays* (New York: Literary Classics, 1998), 12.
15. Ibid., 15.
16. See *Nation of Cowards: Black Activism in Barack Obama's Post-Racial America*.
17. "An Open Statement to the Fans of *The Help*." Association of Black Women

Historians. April 11, 2011, http://www.abwh.org/images/pdf/TheHelp
-Statement.pdf.

18. Kathryn Stockett, *The Help* (New York: Penguin, 2009), 18.
19. Ibid., 19.
20. Ibid.

CHAPTER THREE

1. Toni Morrison at Portland State, May 30, 1975, http://giftedandratchet.com
/2014/07/05/rare-toni-morrison-speech-unearthed.
2. Derrick Bell, *Silent Covenants: Brown V. Board of Education and the Unfulfilled Hopes for Racial Reform* (New York: Oxford University Press, 2004), 81.
3. Ibid.
4. Ibid., my emphasis.
5. Toni Morrison, *Beloved* (New York: Penguin, 1988), 232.
6. *Frederick Douglass: Selected Speeches and Writings,* ed. Philip S. Foner (Chicago: Chicago Review Press, 1999), 193.
7. Morrison, *Beloved*, 190.
8. Ibid.
9. Ibid.
10. "James Baldwin Tells Us All How to Cool It This Summer," *Esquire*, July 1968. http://www.esquire.com/features/james-baldwin-cool-it.
11. Carol Anderson, "Ferguson isn't about black rage against cops. It's about white rage against black progress," *Washington Post*, August 29, 2014, https:// www.washingtonpost.com/opinions/ferguson-wasnt-black-rage-against -copsit-was-white-rage-against-progress/2014/08/29/3055e3f4–2d75–11e4 -bb9b-997ae96fad33_story.html?utm_term=.b007e6f30d8d.
12. Wolf Blitzer interviews Deray McKesson on CNN, April 28, 2015, https:// www.youtube.com/watch?v=NyYdKD0af78.
13. Ibid.
14. "MLK: A Riot Is the Language of the Unheard," CBSNews.Com, August 25, 2013. http://www.cbsnews.com/news/mlk-a-riot-is-the-language-of-the -unheard.
15. Soon after this successful student campaign, which was bolstered signifi- cantly when the black football players signed on and threatened not to play until the president was fired, Missouri legislators proposed a bill that would strip college athletes of their scholarships if they used the threat of not playing as a form of political protest.
16. Two of the four officers that assaulted King were eventually found guilty and subsequently imprisoned by a federal district court. However, Daniel Panta- leo, the officer that strangled Garner to death, will not face federal charges.
17. Ian Haney López, *Dog Whistle Politics* (New York: Oxford University Press, 2015), 51–52.

18. Carol Anderson, *White Rage: The Unspoken Truth of Our Racial Divide* (New York: Bloomsbury Publishing, 2016), 126–35.
19. Michelle Alexander, *The New Jim Crow* (New York: New Press, 2012), 59.
20. Ibid., 84.
21. They admitted as much in an interview with NPR.
22. Andrew Dunn, Mark Washburn, and Michael Gordon, "Shelby police chief describes arrest of Charleston shooting suspect," *Charlotte Observer*, June 19, 2015, http://www.charlotteobserver.com/news/local/article2495 2345.html.
23. Mia De Graaf, "Outrage after Charleston Judge Tells Relatives of Murdered Churchgoers That the Killer's Family Are VICTIMS . . . as it is revealed he was once reprimanded for using the n-word in court." DailyMail.com, June 19, 2015, http://www.dailymail.co.uk/news/article-3132109/Outrage -Charleston-judge-tells-relatives-church-shooting-victims-SYMPATHIZE -killer-s-family-revealed-reprimanded-using-n-word-court.html.
24. Paula Young Lee, "Robert Dear, 'gentle loner': the *New York Times* reveals a load of biases in early round of Colorado Springs Planned Parenthood coverage," Salon.com, November 30, 2015, http://www.salon.com/2015/11/30 /robert_dear_gentle_loner_the_new_york_times_reveals_a_load_of_biases _in_early_round_of_colorado_springs_planned_parenthood_coverage.
25. Ibid.
26. The term was first coined by FBI chief Jim Comey, who made the link based purely on anecdotal evidence. Attorney General Loretta Lynch— whom Comey reports to—discredited the notion during testimony before the House Judiciary Committee, noting that there was no data to back up Comey's claims.
27. When he was arrested, Dylan Roof told the police he was hungry and they provided him with a meal from Burger King.
28. Ta-Nehisi Coates, "Charles Barkley and Plague of 'Unintelligent' Blacks," *Atlantic*, October 28, 2014, http://www.theatlantic.com/politics/archive /2014/10/charles-barkley-and-the-plague-of-unintelligent-blacks/382022/.
29. Ta-Nehisi Coates, "Barack Obama, Ferguson, and the Evidence of Things Unsaid," *Atlantic*, November 26, 2014, http://www.theatlantic.com/politics /archive/2014/11/barack-obama-ferguson-and-the-evidence-of-things-unsaid /383212.
30. Ibid.
31. Ibid.
32. Alexander, *The New Jim Crow*, 180.

CHAPTER FOUR

1. Rosa Parks, *Rosa Parks: My Story* (New York: Penguin, 1992), 116.
2. Rosa Parks expresses deep reservations about King's nonviolent doctrine on a number of occasions in the autobiography. The most illuminating is

when he is punched by a violent white man during a speech and refuses to fight back.

3. Toni Morrison, *Beloved* (New York: Penguin, 1988), 190.

4. Micki McElya, *Clinging to Mammy: The Faithful Slave in Twentieth-Century America* (Cambridge, MA: Harvard University Press, 2007), 6.

5. W. E. B. Du Bois conflates attaining manhood with gaining full recognition of citizenship in the United States. For a more thorough critique of this gendered phenomena see Hazel Carby's *Race Men*.

6. W. E. B. Du Bois, *Souls of Black Folks* (Chicago: Dover Thrift Editions, 1994), 5.

7. Martell Teasley, 2009, conversation.

8. Toni Morrison, *Playing in the Dark: Whiteness and the Literary Imagination* (New York: Random House, 1992), 38.

9. Ibid.

10. Tamar Lewin, "Citing Individualism, Arizona Tries to Rein in Ethnic Studies in School," *New York Times*, May 13, 2010, http://www.nytimes.com/2010 /05/14/education/14arizona.html.

11. Cleve R. Wootson Jr., "A Professor Wants to Teach 'The Problem of Whiteness.' A Lawmaker Calls the Class 'Garbage,'" *Washington Post*, December 28, 2016, https://www.washingtonpost.com/news/grade-point/wp/2016/12/28 /a-professor-wants-to-teach-the-problems-of-whiteness-a-lawmaker-calls -the-class-garbage/?utm_term=.333fc4584644/.

12. Scott Bauer, "Walker Calls 'Whiteness' Class at UW-Madison 'Goofy,'" *Star Tribune*, December 21, 2016, http://www.startribune.com/university-defends -course-on-race-relations/407741896/.

13. James Baldwin, *The Fire Next Time* (New York: Random House, 1993), 87.

14. Coretta Scott King's Funeral. New Birth Baptist Church, Lithonia, Georgia. February 7, 2006.

15. W. E. B. Du Bois, "Criteria for Negro Art," in *Within the Circle: An Anthology of African American Literary Criticism from the Harlem Renaissance to the Present*, ed. Angelyn Mitchell (Durham, NC: Duke University Press, 1994), 66.

16. Ibid., 67.

17. John Horn, Nicole Sperling, and Doug Smith. "Unmasking the Academy: Oscar Voters Overwhelmingly White, Male." *LA Times*, February 19, 2012, http://www.latimes.com/entertainment/la-et-unmasking-oscar-academy -project-20120219-story.html.

18. June Jordan, "Poem for South African Women," in *Directed by Desire: The Collected Poems of June Jordan* (Port Townsend, WA: Copper Canyon Press, 2007), 278.

CHAPTER FIVE

1. I am reminded here of James Baldwin's discussion of the Christ figure and whiteness in *The Fire Next Time*. Baldwin says that as a teenager he intuitively understood that Jesus and God were both white—a cultural reality

that eventually led him away from preaching and adherence to mainstream (white) Christian doctrine.

2. Scott Neuman, "McDonald's Shuts Down Website that Told Workers to Avoid Fast Food," December 26, 2013, NPR, http://www.npr.org/sections /thetwo-way/2013/12/26/257381730/mcdonalds-shuts-website-that-told -employees-to-avoid-fast-food.

3. Adam Mansbach, "The Audacity of Post-racism," in *The Speech: Race and Barack Obama's "A More Perfect Union,"* ed. Tracy Sharpley-Whiting (New York: Bloomsbury, 2009), 69–84.

4. Aisha Harris, "Santa Claus Should Not Be White Any More," *Slate*, December 10, 2013, http://www.slate.com/articles/life.

5. Aisha Harris, "What Fox News Doesn't Understand about Santa Claus." *Slate*, December 12, 2013, http://www.slate.com/blogs/browbeat.

6. *The Kelly File*, December 11, 2013, *The Fox News Channel*.

7. Jon Stewart, *The Daily Show*, on *Comedy Central*, December 12, 2013.

8. Megyn Kelly, *The Kelly File*, on *The Fox News Channel*, December 13, 2013.

9. Robert Jensen, "White Privilege Shapes the U.S.: Affirmative Action for Whites is a Fact of Life," *Baltimore Sun*, July 19, 1998, http://articles.baltimore sun.com/1998–07–19/news/1998200115_1_white-privilege-unearned-white -action-for-whites.

10. Po Bronson and Ashley Merryman, *Nurture Shock* (New York: Hachette Book Group, 2009), 62.

11. Ibid., 64.

12. Ibid., 64.

13. Ibid., 68.

14. Ibid.

15. Ibid.

16. Ibid, 69.

17. Ibid.

18. Ibid.

19. Zora Neale Hurston, *Dust Tracks on a Road* (New York: Harper Collins, 1990), 191.

20. Part of what made Hurston so controversial, besides her before-its-time feminism and inexplicable conservatism, was her critique of colorist politics—a major taboo subject of her day.

21. "Lupita Nyong'o Delivers Moving 'Black Women in Hollywood' Acceptance Speech," *Essence*. February 28, 2014, http://www.essence.com/2014 /02/27/lupita-nyongo-delivers-moving-black-women-hollywood-acceptance -speech/.

22. I discuss these issues in greater depth in my third book, *Blinded by the Whites: Why Race Still Matters in 21st-Century America*.

23. Ta-Nehisi Coates, *Between the World and Me* (New York: Spiegel & Grau, 2015), 7.

CODA

1. Jennifer Agiesta, "Poll: Majority sees Southern Flag as Southern pride symbol, not racist," CNN, 07/ 02/ 2015, http://www.cnn.com/2015/07/02/politics/confederate-flag-poll-racism-southern-pride.
2. On July 9, 2015, South Carolina house legislators voted 94–20 on a proposal to remove the confederate flag from statehouse grounds. It came down the next day.
3. James Baldwin, *The Fire Next Time* (New York: Random House, 1993), 6.
4. Tony Capaccio, "MLK's speech attracted FBI's intense attention," *Washington Post*, August 27, 2013, https://www.washingtonpost.com/politics/mlks-speech-attracted-fbis-intense-attention/2013/08/27/31c8ebd4–0f60–11e3–8cdd-bcdc09410972_story.html.
5. Jim Uhls, *Fight Club*, DVD. Directed by David Fincher (Miami: Fox, 1999).
6. Assata Shakur, "To My People," 07/04/1973, The Talking Drum.com, http://www.thetalkingdrum.com/tmp.html.

Index